D0458930

THE MASK OF KEATS
A STUDY OF PROBLEMS

Books by

ROBERT GITTINGS

JOHN KEATS: THE LIVING YEAR
WENTWORTH PLACE AND OTHER POEMS
FAMOUS MEETING (*Poems Narrative and Lyric*)
THE MAKERS OF VIOLENCE (*A Verse Drama*)
OUT OF THIS WOOD (*A Sequence of Five Plays*)

Cast of the Death Mask of Keats

THE MASK OF KEATS

A STUDY OF PROBLEMS

by

ROBERT GITTINGS

WILLIAM HEINEMANN LTD

MELBOURNE LONDON TORONTO

FIRST PUBLISHED 1956

PRINTED IN GREAT BRITAIN
AT THE WINDMILL PRESS
KINGSWOOD, SURREY

To

H. W. GARROD

CONTENTS

ILLUSTRATIONS

FOREWORD

SINCE the publication, two years ago, of my *John Keats: The Living Year*, it has been suggested that I should attempt to deal with some problems in Keats's life and work which were either not treated fully in my previous book or were outside its time-scheme. In this first category were the debt of Keats to his reading of Dante and the exact date of his composition of the sonnet *Bright Star*; both of these I have dealt with at some length here. The other studies in this book are concerned with a variety of subjects, both biographical and literary, concerned with Keats. All have this in common, that there has hitherto been considerable doubt and discrepancy in the evidence and conclusion about them. I do not claim to have solved all these problems—indeed many, like most human affairs, are incapable of any exact solution—but I hope that these attempts to do so may bring readers nearer to Keats, and to look more closely behind the mask that time and some degree of misconception has placed between us and the most rewarding and human of poets.

Each of these studies is dedicated to someone who, in his or her way, has advanced our knowledge of Keats. Where these have supplied fresh material as the basis of these studies, their names will also be found among the Acknowledgments; but none is to be held responsible for the arguments or the conclusions of any study so inscribed.

ACKNOWLEDGMENTS

THE author's thanks are due to Mrs. Sowerby for permission to reproduce as frontispiece a photograph of the death-mask of John Keats, now in the possession of the Meynell family and at present on exhibition at Offord and Meynell, booksellers, Chichester; to Louis M. Rabinowitz of New York for permission to reproduce photographs of Keat's copy of Dante's *Inferno*, now in his possession; to the late H. C. Brooke-Taylor for permission to use and quote letters to John Taylor, Keats's publisher, from the Taylor family papers at Bakewell, Derbyshire; to Miss Mabel A. E. Steele, Librarian of the Houghton Library, Harvard, for permission to reprint my essay "Keats and Chatterton" from *The Keats-Shelley Journal of America* and to quote part of a letter; also to Mr. Donald Parson for permission to quote this letter from his book *Portraits of Keats*; to Miss Alyse Gregory for permission to quote a passage from Llewellyn Powys's *Dorset Essays*; to Canon Herbert Pentin, part-author of *Memorials of Old Dorset*; to the Directors of the British Museum for permission to reproduce a photograph of a portion of Keats's MS. of *Hyperion*; to George Morey, Ph.D.; to J. H. Preston, Assistant Curator of Keats House, Hampstead, for his unfailing help; to Mr. John Gittings for his care in checking the typescript and proofs of Appendix A; to Miss Joan P. Kettle for preparing the typescript for the press; and to my wife.

R. G.

1

DEATH MASK AND PORTRAIT

To Vivian Meynell

THE life-mask of Keats, taken by B. R. Haydon, is well known. The death-mask of Keats, which was taken in Rome, possibly by Gherardi, the mask-maker to Canova, is considerably less well known. Indeed, it is not too much to say that it is comparatively unfamiliar, even to Keats scholars. The reason for this is difficult to understand. Admittedly, the cast taken by Haydon has been preserved in Keats House, Hampstead, and therefore is familiar, either in itself or in copies, to all Keats's lovers. On the other hand, the original matrix of the death-mask, sent by Severn to John Taylor, and bought in 1865, after the latter's death, by Lord Houghton, seems to have disappeared. Yet a plaster cast was taken from this matrix, and sold up to 1921 and perhaps later, first at 2s. 6d. and then at 5s. od., by C. Smith of London. It is therefore remarkable that there should be such a scarcity of copies of this cast that they hardly ever appear, and the appearance of one is a matter of interest. Thanks to the kindness of Mr. Vivian Meynell, grandson of Wilfrid and Alice Meynell, I have been able to examine carefully one of these casts, which has been in the possession of the family for at least forty years. Its condition suggests one reason why so few casts have survived. It has evidently been broken at one time. One imagines that Victorian dustbins contained many plaster fragments of Keats. The Meynell cast has, however, been skilfully mended, and the crack, caused by loose plaster falling out of the break, has been carefully filled in. Nothing has been lost except for some letters of the cast-making firm's name and address—for instance, the initial "S" of the word "Smith"—engraved at the top rim of the cast, near to a hook which has been inserted for hanging it on the wall.

The cast, worn and scratched by time, has paradoxically an extremely lifelike look. It shows a complete correspondence with all features of the life-mask, except that suffering has drawn back the sensitive nostrils, and engraved a deep line between each of them and the corners of the mouth. The jaw, too, has fallen in death, though the effect of this is lessened by the linen grave-cloth which holds it up, and whose faint line can be seen imprinted in the cast, beneath the chin and up either cheek to the top of the head where it was tied. Yet the face, though marked by long illness, is still strangely alive, and has much of what we associate with the living Keats.

This association may perhaps be accounted for by the fact that one of the portraits of Keats, with which we are most familiar, was not painted from life at all, but from the original of this death-mask. It has never, I think, been pointed out before that the full-length picture by Severn in the National Portrait Gallery is a portrait not of a live but of a dead man; yet such is the case. This portrait, with all its circumstantial detail of Keats reading in his Hampstead room—a copy by Edmund Dyer hangs in the room itself—was nevertheless painted after Keats's death. Moreover, it was painted immediately after his death, and taken from the casts of Keats's head, hand and foot, which were preserved by Severn for Taylor. A letter of Severn to Taylor, dated 16 May 1821, makes this clear.

> I have begun a small whole length of him—from last seeing him at Hampstead—this I will finish and send to you—I have likewise a drawing taken in middle of night with the cold sweat on his face—about 3 Weeks before his death—The casts I must send another time—because I still require them to finish the picture from—

Once one realises this, the extraordinary character of the portrait becomes clear. The face and the right hand are those of a dead man. This is most noticeable when one isolates the hand, which lies upon the pages of the open book with a dead weight entirely unlike life. Severn was not a skilful enough artist merely to use the casts as suggestions for his imaginary study; he transferred their features, particular to the dead man, into the living image. So, in the supposedly live face of the poet, we have the drawn lines and the retracted nostrils of the face in death, as perfectly shown when the plaster cast is photographed at approximately the same angle as it was portrayed in the picture by Severn.

The Meynell cast, which conclusively proves this point, also decides a question which has been the subject of some debate—the authenticity of the cast in the possession of J. H. Preston, Assistant Curator of Keats Memorial House, Hampstead. This cast has been bronzed over and very considerably polished; this has caused it to look, particularly in photographic reproductions, somewhat unlike Keats in certain features. Owing to these circumstances, a doubt has arisen about its authenticity, with results which include the following letter from Miss Mabel A. E. Steele, Custodian of the Keats Collection in the Houghton Library at Harvard University, reproduced in Mr. Donald Parson's valuable work, *Portraits of Keats*.

> In the summer of 1950 the director of this library, Mr. William A. Jackson, was in London with authority to purchase the death mask of Keats at Hampstead if he found it authentic. While he was there a letter was published in *The Times Literary Supplement*, June 30th, 1950, p. 405, signed by three granddaughters of Joseph Severn, Margaret Birkenhead, C. H. Furneaux and Joan Smith, who stated that they had known as children, and frequently seen, the original death mask of Keats, when it was in the possession of their mother in their house at Oxford. They wrote, in part: "having studied the photograph of the cast . . . generally supposed to be of Keats, which was published in Mr. Neville Rogers' book of *Keats, Shelley and Rome*, we are of the definite opinion that this bears no resemblance to the original death mask."

As a result of this situation, the cast was not bought for Harvard, but remains in Mr. Preston's possession. A comparison between it and the Meynell cast, however, now shows that they undoubtedly come from the same matrix. Since the Meynell cast, as has been said, displays such a strong correspondence with the features both of the Haydon life-mask and of the National Portrait Gallery painting, there can be no doubt that the cast at Hampstead is of Keats, though it is easy to see how a photographic reproduction could mislead even Severn's own descendants. The camera is particularly prone to lie when it foreshortens rounded surfaces, and it is therefore unfortunate that the photograph of the Preston cast, alluded to on page 3, was apparently taken full-face, the effect being to alter the shape of lips and nose, which are far more fairly reproduced in a profile study; such a study also has the advantage of providing an easy comparison with the one real test of authenticity, the National Gallery Portrait, which, as we have seen, is a true portrait, and the only one that exists, of the original matrix of Keats's death-mask.

2

KEAT'S DEBT TO DANTE

To Louis M. Rabinowitz

I

KEATS'S copy of Dante's *Inferno*, containing his markings and underlinings, provides an opportunity to study his own work in a way that has not been afforded before by any other relic of the poet. Keats, it is true, had the habit of marking extensively where he read, and many of the books he treated in this way are fortunately still in existence—his folio Shakespeare, his *Paradise Lost*, and the second volume of Burton's *The Anatomy of Melancholy* at the Keats Museum, Hampstead; his seven-volume 12mo. Shakespeare and the first volume of *The Faerie Queene* at Harvard.

Yet the markings in the Dante are unique, in that we can relate them positively to exact phases of Keats's own work, and to the times when he himself was composing particular poems. His references to Shakespeare, Milton, Burton and Spenser are scattered throughout his letters in a general way; we cannot, except in rare instances, relate them in detail to any one time in his life, though, particularly with Burton, we can deduce from Keats's letters a fairly accurate sequence of his reading. Keats's references to his reading of Dante's *Inferno*, however, are few and precise. We know exactly when he started reading this particular volume, and we can pick up the thread of his reading from the other references. Since his markings in the text fall into three clearly-defined groups, we can date each one, and find its influence on whatever poem or group of poems he was composing at the time.

It follows that anyone who attempts a study of Keats's work by these means owes a very special debt to someone who has accurately transcribed Keats's markings in the *Inferno*. It is a pleasure to be able to pay tribute to the generosity and helpful enthusiasm of the owner of Keats's copy of the *Inferno*, Mr. Louis M. Rabinowitz of New York. Not only has he assisted me in every way in all enquiries I have made about the volume; he has personally transcribed and checked all the markings made by Keats in it, and supplied me with the excellent photographs which are reproduced here by his kind permission. In every way this volume, which was so close to Keats in his lifetime, has found a worthy and appreciative owner in our own.

A copy of Dante's *Inferno* is mentioned in the list of Keats's books, made a few months after the poet's death by his friend, Charles Armitage Brown. This copy has disappeared; if it were to come to light, it might well be of interest. It was the translation made by the Rev. H. F. Cary and published by J. Carpenter in 1805, in two volumes octavo, and listed thus by Brown. Brown, who regarded himself as Keats's literary executor, drew up this list in order to carry out the brief provision of Keats's Will—"My Chest of Books divide among my friends." His system was to give back to the donors any books they had given to Keats, to return any lent books, and to give the rest to those friends he thought would appreciate the gift most. He added a list of these friends, including himself, amounting to eighteen in all, with a number against each name. There are also numbers against some of the books, and some have the small letter "m", almost certainly standing for "me" or "mine"—that is, the books that Brown kept for himself. That the numbers, where they occur, correspond to the numbered list of friends is evident. For instance, the number 5 is placed against a copy of Tasso's poems. No. 5 on the list of friends is Charles Cowden Clarke, whose love of Tasso was celebrated in verse by Keats, and who was obviously the recipient of this volume.

Against the two-volume Dante occur both the letter "m" and the number 11. Brown, who regarded these books as souvenirs of his dead friend rather than reading matter, often split up editions of more than one volume in this way. No. 11 in the list of friends, and therefore the recipient of one of these odd volumes, was Mrs. Isabella Jones, the beautiful and enigmatic lady on whose suggestion Keats had written *The Eve of St. Agnes*. This does not, however, prove either that she had originally given the *Inferno* to Keats, or that she was considered a particularly appropriate person to receive it. Her name is substituted in the list for that of Charles Lamb, the original number 11. Lamb's love of Dante was well known, and it is probable that Brown first selected the *Inferno* for him, and then, considering Mrs. Jones a closer friend of the poet, substituted her name.

There was, however, another copy of the *Inferno* possessed by Keats, though not at this time in his "Chest of Books". In 1814, Cary had completed his translation of the whole of the Divine Comedy, and had published it in three minute 32mo. volumes "printed for the Author by J. Barfield". Four years later, in 1818, this edition came to the enthusiastic notice of Samuel Taylor Coleridge. Coleridge quoted it in his lectures, and persuaded Taylor & Hessey, Keats's publishers, to take over the remaining 650 copies of the 1814 edition and to send them out under their imprint. Although neither publishers nor readers liked the tiny size of the volumes—they measure only 4½ by 2¾ inches—the edition sold out within a year, to make way for one of a more reasonable format.

The size of the little edition commended itself to Keats for a special reason. Just when it came out, in June 1818, he was going on a walking-tour with Brown in the Lake District and in Scotland. These small books would fit into his knapsack. A joking message to Hessey, just as he was setting off—"I hope he'll *Carey* his point"—shows that he had been given the books by his publishers, who were generous of free copies to their young poet, while another joking remark in a letter to his brother George a week later, when he refers to "Correspondence printed as close as the Apostles creed in a Watchpaper", may indicate that he, like other readers, found the miniature print rather hard going. This copy of the *Inferno*, with its two companion volumes, seems to have remained in Keats's hands from June 1818 until at least the second week in October 1819. After that, or perhaps at about that time, it passed into the hands of Miss Fanny Brawne, to whom Keats was by then formally engaged.

The exact date and circumstances under which she received it are unknown. There is no inscription from him to her, as there is on the fly-leaf of the folio of Shakespeare's plays, now in the Keats Museum, Hampstead. On the front inner cover of the *Inferno* there is, however, an inscription of great interest, and one which may help to date Fanny Brawne's possession of the volume. This is a version of Keats's *Bright Star* sonnet in her handwriting. The version has been known, but the handwriting has never been reproduced before. Although clearly hers, it is different in many ways from the two groups of her writing which have already been reproduced at various times. One is the very immature hand of some entries which she made, early in 1819, in the copy of Leigh Hunt's *Literary Pocket Book* now in the Keats Museum; the other is the much more mature and assured hand in which she wrote, from September 1820 onwards, her letters to Fanny Keats, also in the Keats Museum.

The handwriting of the sonnet, though it has many characteristics of both the other groups, is far more mature than the first and not so formed as the second. It contains some of the carelessness that mars Fanny Brawne's earlier writing; it seems somewhat casual, for instance, to begin line 3 with "&" instead of the fully-written "And". On the other hand, the formation of most of the letters is much more like her 1820 writing. It may very well belong to a period about mid-way between the two, that is, late in 1819. Keats had written a first version of this sonnet a year earlier, in October 1818; but that this is the version finally approved by him is shown by the fact that Fanny Brawne's copy is identical, in all but the smallest points of spelling and punctuation, with the only copy known to exist in the poet's handwriting.

The later history of the book cannot be dated with even this degree of accuracy, but the main facts are clear. Sometime between 1901 and 1906, the volumes passed into the hands of Harry Buxton Forman, who used Fanny Brawne's manuscript to collate his printing of the *Bright Star* sonnet in the Oxford edition of Keats's poems. His preface to this edition is dated October 1906, and speaks of the Dante being in his possession. Between 1917 and 1920, it passed into the hands of T. J. Wise. In his Catalogue of the Ashley Library, Vol. III (1923), Wise printed a long but in many ways inaccurate description of the Dante. At some unknown date between 1923 and 1937, Wise sold the Dante to the American collector, A. E. Newton. At the sale of Newton's collection in 1941, it passed into the hands

Bright star! would I were stedfast as thou art
Not in lone splendour hung aloft the night
& watching with eternal lids apart
Like nature's patient sleepless eremite
The moving waters at their priest-like task
Of pure ablution round earth's human shores;
Or gazing on the new soft-fallen masque
Of snow upon the mountains & the moors.
No! yet still stedfast, still unchangeable
Pillowed upon my fair love's ripening breast
To feel for ever its soft swell & fall
Awake for ever in a sweet unrest
Still still to hear her tender-taken breath
And so live ever or else swoon to death

'Bright Star' in Fanny Brawne's Handwriting

2

I journey'd on over that lonely steep,
The hinder foot still firmer. Scarce the ascent
Began, when, lo! a panther, nimble, light, 30
And cover'd with a speckled skin, appear'd,
Nor, when it saw me, vanish'd, rather strove
To check my onward going; that ofttimes
With purpose to retrace my steps I turn'd.
The hour was morning's prime, and on his way 35
Aloft the sun ascended with those stars,
That with him rose, when Love divine first mov'd
Those its fair works: so that with joyous hope
All things conspir'd to fill me, the gay skin
Of that swift animal, the matin dawn 40
And the sweet season. Soon that joy was chas'd,
And by new dread succeeded, when in view
A lion came, 'gainst me, as it appear'd,
With his head held aloft and hunger-mad,
That e'en the air was fear-struck. A she-wolf 45
Was at his heels, who in her leanness seem'd
Full of all wants, and many a land hath made
Disconsolate ere now. She with such fear
O'erwhelmed me, at the sight of her appall'd,
That of the height all hope I lost. As one, 50
Who with his gain elated, sees the time
When all unwares is gone, he inwardly
Mourns with heart-griping anguish; such was I,
Haunted by that fell beast, never at peace,
Who coming o'er against me, by degrees 55
Impell'd me where the sun in silence rests.
While to the lower space with backward step
I fell, my ken discern'd the form of one,
Whose voice seem'd faint through long disuse of speech.
When him in that great desert I espied, 60
"Have mercy on me!" cried I out aloud,
"Spirit! or living man! whate'er thou be!"

PAGE 2 OF DANTE'S 'INFERNO'
MARKED BY KEATS

of A. W. Rosenbach, and in 1947 it was bought by the present owner, Mr. Louis M. Rabinowitz. Both Wise and the Newton sale catalogue published photographs, but the illustrations given here, both of the *Bright Star* sonnet and of Keats's actual markings in the text of the *Inferno*, have never appeared anywhere before.

There is no doubt that the markings made in ink in the text of the *Inferno* volume are from Keats's pen. They are, in fact, in every way his characteristic system of marking a book. Writing about his own epic poem *Hyperion* to John Hamilton Reynolds, Keats said:

> It may be interesting to you to pick out some lines from Hyperion and put a mark X to the false beauty proceeding from art, and one || to the true voice of feeling.

Something of the same system was pursued by Keats when he perceived "the true voice of feeling" in another writer, and extended it to emphasise different degrees of approval, by single, double, or even treble line-markings, both underlining or in the margin. His markings are a sort of literary Baedeker, or perhaps more accurately like those of a Government Whip, one, two, or three lines in ascending order of importance. They can most fruitfully be seen in his copy of Volume II of Burton's *The Anatomy of Melancholy* and in *Troilus and Cressida* in his folio Shakespeare, both in the Keats Museum. In these markings, we can actually see how poetry affected Keats, and what, in his opinion, it should be. They are the spontaneous response to that quality of poetry which, in his own words, "should surprise by a fine excess."

One great value of this volume of the *Inferno*, then, is that it enables us to see poetry through Keats's eyes. A general view of the markings shows how unerring his poetical instinct was. Cary's translation, though a great achievement whose standard of performance seldom flags, is not an inspired piece of work. The mild blank verse, into which he has translated Dante's terza rima, is like that of a less-inspired Milton, and Keats's reading of it may account in part for the "Miltonic inversions" which he condemned in his own *Hyperion*. Yet Cary rises to the great moments of the epic, which, for most readers, is the main thing; at these moments he can hardly have had a more appreciative reader than Keats. Keats noted in the margin of his copy of *Paradise Lost*, probably during his enthusiastic re-reading of that poem in August 1819,

> There is always a great charm in the openings of great poems where the action begins—that of Dante's Hell.

He showed this spirit by marking the first two pages of the first canto of the *Inferno* more heavily than anywhere else. For his warmest appreciation—two lines below the phrase and three in the margin—he singled out Cary's specially felicitous description of the She-Wolf as "Full of all wants". It is a phrase that one does not perhaps pick out until Keats has done so, but then the soundness of his instinct is apparent. Again he showed a lively and immediate enthusiasm for what he described, once more in the margin of his *Paradise Lost*, as "the brief pathos of Dante". The *Inferno* is full of short and lovely passages which relieve the horror and bitterness of much of the work. They almost always bring a real strain of poetry from Cary, upon which Keats pounced with evident joy. He marked with special emphasis the beautiful image, which partly lightens by its loveliness the torment of the sinners in the burning sand of Canto xiv—

> Dilated flakes of fire, as flakes of snow
> On Alpine summit, when the wind is hush'd.

For this, as will be seen, he tried to find a parallel image of beauty in his own *Hyperion*. He showed too an appreciation of those passages of natural description, which are too often missed in some of the grotesque and unnatural horrors contrived by Dante's imagination. Typical of this is his heavy marking of a passage in Canto xxvi, which in its turn had some influence on his own *Ode to Autumn*.

> As in that season, when the sun least veils
> His face that lightens all, what time the fly
> Gives way to the shrill gnat, the peasant then
> Upon some cliff reclin'd, beneath him sees
> Fire-flies innumerous spangling o'er the vale,
> Vineyard or tilth, where his day-labour lies:

This influence on his own poems, indeed, shows that there is a second and even more important aspect of Keats's markings. T. J. Wise speaks in his Ashley Catalogue of Keats "marking many passages to draw her (Fanny Brawne's) attention to them". Apart from the fact that he marked the majority of these passages before he had met Fanny Brawne, the idea shows a complete lack of knowledge of Keats's way of work. A highly important part of all Keats's intense reading was what he himself called "study". By this, he meant the deliberate and concentrated reading of a work in order to fit himself for a particular composition of his own. For example, he wrote the heroic couplets of *Lamia* "after much study of Dryden's versification", and there are other instances of this fastening his attention on an author in order to derive the greatest possible sustenance for his own work.

One point about this should be made clear. When a poet does this—and Keats was by no means the only poet who has gone to work in this way—there is no suggestion of imitation or plagiarism, and the result which he produces is in no way a mere pastiche, but a living and original work. In fact, it is the sign of a great artist in any sphere to be able to transcend his material, to be able to stand up to the greatest possible works in his own medium, and to transmute what he extracts from them into something quite new and characteristic of his own art. It is only the second-rate artist who is swamped by what he reads or sees, and who falls back on imitation. It is the measure of the great artist that he can assimilate and use the greatest.

That is what appears from Keats's reading of the *Inferno*. He was consciously fitting himself for writing an epic and philosophic poem, *Hyperion*, by reading an epic and philosophic poem of the highest class. All Keats's letters from the time that he conceives the idea of *Hyperion* early in 1818 show a desire to put himself in touch with philosophic literature. He discusses in an extremely perceptive way the relative positions of Milton and Wordsworth as epic and philosophic poets in a letter to Reynolds of May 3rd, 1818, just before he had begun reading Dante, and concludes

> We read fine things but never feel them to the full until we have gone the same steps as the Author.

As we study Keats's reading of Dante through his markings in this volume, we too can in some degree go the same steps as Keats. We are presented with the spectacle of a great poet grappling with the finest work of another great poet, and subduing it to his own appreciative and creative impulses. In a unique way we are in touch with a poet's actual method of work. However much we know, we can never explain or exactly account for this way of work; but with such material as this volume at hand, we may get some hint or perception of the process. Keats's markings in the *Inferno* fall into three very clearly-defined groups. The first consists of the extensive markings in Canto i; then, after seven unmarked cantos, there is a marked group of Cantos ix to xv, and finally, after another six unmarked, a third group from Canto xxii to xxvii. Each one of these, together with a re-reading mentioned in his letters, is associated with a particular phase in his own creative life, and their detailed study is the subject of the four sections that follow.

II

Since Keats's reading of the *Inferno* has, as its chief fruits, his own composition of the two unfinished attempts at the epic theme of *Hyperion*, we may start by looking at the origins of that work. A racy account is given in the circumstantial but usually inaccurate reminiscences of Joseph Severn the painter, who was with Keats when he died. Writing nearly a quarter of a century after Keats's death, Severn says:

> I recollect at this moment the origin of the Hyperion.—Keats was abusing Milton to me & a f^{d} whose name I forget, but who was rather stern—I had expressed my great admiration & delight in Milton, when this f^{d} turning to Keats said "Keats I think it great reproach to you that Severn should admire & appreceate Milton & you a poet should know nothing of him, for you confess never to have read him, therefore your dislike goes for nothing"—after this Keats took up Milton & became an ardent admirer and soon began the Hyperion.

Severn's exuberant memory was always apt to telescope events, and it is unlikely that this exact scene ever took place. He is accurate, however, in his account of the part played by the friend "who was rather stern". This was Benjamin Bailey, afterwards Archdeacon of Colombo, who was reading for Holy Orders at Oxford when Keats first knew him. Keats went to stay with Bailey at Magdalen College in September 1817, and was there introduced to Milton's works by his host, who regarded himself as an authority on epic poetry.

Early in 1818 Keats was planning *Hyperion*, which was to be an epic poem and an advance on the "romance" of *Endymion*, which he was just seeing through the press. Bailey had obtained a curacy near Carlisle, though he was still finishing his terms at Oxford. In May he reviewed the recently-published *Endymion*, and asked Keats to come and stay with him again. A month earlier, however, Keats had decided on a different way of spending the summer; in his own words,

> to put my knapsack at my back and make a pedestrian tour through the North of England, and part of Scotland—to make a sort of Prologue to the Life I intend to pursue—that is to write, to study and to see all Europe at the lowest expence.

He also wished to see as much as possible of his brother George, who was about to marry and emigrate to America. He therefore had to refuse Bailey's invitation, though promising to try and call on him in his northern curacy. Bailey, his eye still on the good that he might do to the young epic poet, had sent Keats a quotation from Dante, and recommended him to read the Divine Comedy. Keats replied:

> I am not at home and your letter being there I cannot look it over to answer any particular—only I must say I felt that passage of Dante—if I take any book with me it shall be those minute volumes of Carey for they will go into the aptest corner.

Bailey followed this by repeating his recommendation, and quoting another passage of the *Inferno*. This letter was forwarded to Keats while actually on his Scottish walking-tour, and he replied:

> You say I must study Dante—well the only Books I have with me are those three little Volumes. I read that fine passage you mention a few days ago.

The serious-minded Bailey can therefore be regarded as the godfather of Keats's reading of the *Inferno* for the serious purpose of providing a background to his own prospective epic of *Hyperion*; it will be noticed that both he and Keats use the word "study" in this connection. For this reason, it would be most interesting to know which passage of Dante it was that Bailey first quoted to Keats, and which Keats felt so deeply that he determined to take Cary's translation with him. Keats's markings in the first half of Canto i of the *Inferno* are remarkably extensive; nearly every line is marked, many with an emphasis which he hardly ever again displays in his reading of the work. It is evident that he was deeply stirred; it is evident too that this first set of markings is most likely to have been made before he started on his tour. They show a deliberation and a selection in his degrees of appreciative signs that he could scarcely have achieved once the strenuous walking-tour was started.

It is most likely that Bailey's initial quotation too came from this first canto. It would have chimed so exactly with Keats's mood at that time. He too, poetically, was

In the midway of this our mortal life,

for he had been writing seriously for just over three years, and had, though he could not know it, less than three years more to live. His brother Tom's illness, now taking a sinister turn, and his brother George's emigration, had forced his thoughts at this exact time to death and the mutability of human affairs. In his letters to Bailey he describes this as producing a lethargy, dullness, and confused state of mind, most like that in which Dante describes himself at the opening of his vision:

How first I entered it I scarce can say,
Such sleepy dulness in that instant weigh'd
My senses down,

The phrases Keats uses—"such a Lethargy", "so depressed", "the pain of existence", "Life must be undergone"—all form a picture of a mental state in which Dante's opening canto would strike deeply into his imagination. Once, he says, he would have hoped to have relieved Bailey's "dullness" by his own high spirits; now he cannot feel this. Whenever he is alone he feels instead "the glory of dying for a great human purpose". Great poems are often conceived, in their mood and colour, at a very different time from either their actual composition or the moment when their story is selected. Keats had settled on the story of *Hyperion* some four months before, and was not to write its first line until some four months later; but it is most likely that here, on a first reading of the poem recommended by Bailey, in tune with his own brooding sense of the human problem, Keats caught the solemn and new note on which he eventually started his great attempt at the epic.

How much he seriously read Dante on his walking-tour is uncertain. He walked large distances over rough country which left him exhausted nearly every evening, and he was companioned by the Rabelaisian and not at all serious-minded Charles Armitage Brown. It is Brown who gives a clue that Keats reading during the six-weeks' tour consisted of just those seven unmarked cantos which follow his intensive marking of Canto i. Writing to Charles Wentworth Dilke, senior, of Chichester, on August 7th, Brown says:

> Then, be it known, in the first place, we are in as continued a bustle as an old Dowager at Home. Always moving—moving from one place to another like Dante's inhabitants of the Sulphur Kingdom in search of cold ground—

Now in the *Inferno*, as Brown must have known unless he was speaking loosely, Dante and his guide Virgil do not reach any region of heat until Canto ix, when they enter into the City of Dis itself, with its burning tombs in which the Heretics are punished. By contrast, in Cantos ii to viii they pass through almost every other element in their journey through the first five circles of Hell—wind, rain, hail, snow, mud, and water. Poor Keats indeed had himself passed through most of these elements on the tour, had contracted a severe sore throat, and was about to leave Brown and return alone by a smack from Inverness to London. He himself uses the word "Sulphur" and images of burning in a humorous poem to Tom written from Inverness at this exact time. It seems that he was at leisure, enforced by illness, for more exact reading and marking, which he recommenced with Canto ix, and that Cantos ii to viii do represent his reading while on tour.

There are, in fact, some small indications scattered throughout his letters and poems that this was so. On July 1st he wrote at Dumfries a sonnet, which he describes as being composed "in a strange mood", on visiting the tomb of Burns, where

> The short-liv'd, paly Summer is but won
> From Winter's ague, for one hour's gleam;
> Though sapphire warm, their Stars do never beam,
> All is Cold Beauty; pain is never done
> For who has mind to relish Minos-wise,
> The real of Beauty, free from that dead hue
> Sickly imagination and sick pride
> Cast wan upon it!

At the beginning of Canto v of the *Inferno*, Dante comes to a place "where no light shines". This is the second circle of the Carnal Sinners, and at its entrance stands Minos.

> There Minos stands
> Grinning with ghastly feature: he, of all
> Who enter, strict examining the crimes,
> Gives sentence and dismisses them beneath,

Here, "Minos-wise", he condemns among others those whose romantic love now ends in their punishment in the second circle, and whose beauty led them to this fate. Keats associates this kind of fate with "the fate of Burns. Poor unfortunate fellow—his disposition was Southern——", as he muses a few days later. Yet, however miserable their ultimate reward for it, men must make their sensual discoveries:

> yet who would not like to discover once again that Cleopatra was a Gipsey, Helen a Rogue and Ruth a deep one?

Here a later section of the same Canto v was still in his mind, where Dante gives a catalogue of the Carnal Sinners:

> Then follows Cleopatra, lustful queen."
> There marked I Helen . . .

This aspect of Burns is still obsessing him when he writes about the visit to the birthplace some days later—"What were his addresses to Jean in the latter part of his life——". It is clear that the history of Burns and that of the sinners in Canto v mingle in his mind, and produce some of the strange sensation of the sonnet, its "cold Beauty".

Other resemblances between what he writes and what he reads are only minor and verbal at this time. On July 10th he wrote his brother Tom "a galloway song" in a not very successful imitation of Burns. It contains a curious image

> His long hair rustled like a flame
> On board a shallop.

This may have something to do with the flame-signal that greets Dante and Virgil across the water at the beginning of Canto viii, and the swift boat that comes to ferry them. Again, a week later, he writes to Tom his comic sonnet, describing some travelling-players performing Kotzebue's *The Stranger* to a bagpipe accompaniment—

> The Stranger next with head on bosom bent
> Sigh'd; rueful again the piteous bagpipe went
> Again the Stranger sighings fresh did waste.

This has some echo of the lines, also from Canto viii, where Virgil is at first refused admittance to the City of Dis.

> Upon the ground
> His eyes were bent, and from his brow eras'd
> All confidence, while thus with sighs he spake:

It was only a few days later that Keats wrote assuring Bailey he had been reading Dante "a few days ago".

It seems likely, however, that the reading of the *Inferno*, begun so enthusiastically on Bailey's recommendation before the tour, and signalled by the first group of markings, was only spasmodic during the tour, and was not taken up again until the second week in August when Keats found himself on his way back to his home in Hampstead. It was there that his second set of markings (Cantos ix to xv) were made, and *Hyperion* itself was begun.

III

Keats announced that he had begun composing his own epic poem, *Hyperion*, on September 20th, 1818, in a letter to Charles Wentworth Dilke, who had gone to the south coast for his health. In giving his friend all the news from Hampstead, Keats wrote

> I was going to Town tomorrow with Mrs. D. but I though(t) it best to ask her excuse this morning—I wish I could say Tom was any better. His identity presses upon me so all day that I am obliged to go out—and although I intended to have given some time to study alone I am obliged to write, and plunge into abstract images to ease myself of his countenance his voice and feebleness—

That is to say, Keats had been forced, by the unbearable presence of his brother's ill-health, to give up the deliberate course of reading he had set himself, and to begin composition of his own poem.

There are many hints in this very letter to show what that course of reading had been. There is a quotation from *Paradise Lost* and another from a sonnet of Ronsard, and both Milton and Ronsard undoubtedly play their part in Keats's poem. Yet in an earlier section of the letter, there is a direct reference to the *Inferno*, and, perhaps, an indirect glance at that particular miniature volume he was reading. Keats, writing facetiously to cheer up his convalescent friend, said:

> . . . how can I with any face begin without a dissertation on letter writing—Yet when I consider that a sheet of paper contains room only for three pages, and a half how can I do justice to such a pregnant subject? however as you have seen the history of the world stamped as it were by a diminishing glass in the form of a chronological Map, so will I 'with retractile claws' draw this in to the form of a table—whereby it will occupy merely the remainder of this first page—

That Keats had been reading his little volume, "stamped as it were by a diminishing glass", is made clear by the quotation.

It is part of the description of the monster Geryon, who in Canto xvii conveys Dante and Virgil down from the seventh to the eighth circle of Hell. In Cary's translation

> Thus, like an eel, outstretch'd at length he steer'd,
> Gath'ring the air up with retractile claws.

Keats had evidently reached this point in his reading by September 20th. He made no markings in Canto xvii nor in the canto which precedes it; but the previous seven cantos, ix to xv, form the second and longest of the three marked sections in his volume. It is evident that here was a main source of "study" to prepare himself for his own *Hyperion*. In fact, it may well be reckoned the prime source; for it is in the opening twenty-one lines of that poem that the influence of these cantos is dominant.

> Deep in the shady sadness of a vale
> Far sunken from the healthy breath of morn,
> Far from the fiery noon, and eve's one star,
> Sat grey-hair'd Saturn, quiet as a stone,
> Still as the silence round about his lair;
> Forest on forest hung above his head
> Like cloud on cloud. No stir of air was there,
> Not so much life as on a summer's day
> Robs not one light seed from the feather'd grass,
> But where the dead leaf fell, there did it rest.
> A stream went voiceless by, still deaden'd more
> By reason of his fallen divinity
> Spreading a shade: the Naiad 'mid her reeds
> Press'd her cold finger closer to her lips.
>
> Along the margin-sand large foot-marks went,
> No further than to where his feet had stray'd,
> And slept there since. Upon the sodden ground
> His old right hand lay nerveless, listless, dead,
> Unsceptred; and his realmless eyes were closed;
> While his bow'd head seem'd list'ning to the Earth,
> His ancient mother, for some comfort yet.

In Canto xiii of the *Inferno*, Dante and Virgil enter the second ring of the seventh circle; this is the dismal wood of those who have committed violence against their own person, the suicides. Virgil speaks of it in the previous canto, and in a passage which Keats marked, as "the gloomy vale", and it is described at the beginning of Canto xiii in another marked passage:

> We enter'd on a forest where no track
> Of steps had worn a way. Not verdant there
> The foliage, but of dusky hue; not light
> The boughs and tapering, but with knares deform'd
> And matted thick:

It is not, however, until Canto xiv that the likeness between this forest valley and Saturn's becomes exact. In this and in Canto xv, all heavily marked by Keats, Dante describes the third ring, containing those who have committed violence against God, Nature, and Art. These lie through another part of the dark wood in a place of burning sand. Dante and Virgil can only go near them by walking between the wood and the hot sand along the "duri margini", or as Cary translates it "the solid margins", which Keats, in his turn, has translated into the magnificently Shakespearean compound "the margin-sand". This is how Keats marked the opening of Canto xiv:

> Soon as the charity of native land
> Wrought in my bosom, I the scatter'd leaves
> Collected, and to him restor'd, who now
> Was hoarse with utt'rance. To the limit thence
> We came, which from the third the second round
> Divides, and where of justice is display'd
> Contrivance horrible. Things then first seen
> Clearlier to manifest, I tell how next
> A plain we reach'd, that from its steril bed
> Each plant repell'd. The mournful wood waves round
> Its garland on all sides, as round the wood
> Spreads the sad foss. There, on the very edge,
> Our steps we stay'd. It was an area wide
> Of arid sand and thick, resembling most
> The soil that erst by Cato's foot was trod.
> Vengeance of Heav'n! Oh! how shouldst thou be fear'd

Hyperion Book 1st

Deep in the shady sadness of a Vale,
Far sunken from the healthy breath of Morn,
Far from the fiery noon, and ~~evening~~ Eve's one star,
Sat grey hair'd Saturn quiet as a Stone,
Still as the silence, round about his Lair.
Forest on forest hung above his head
~~Like Clouds that whose bosoms thundrous bosoms~~
Like Cloud on Cloud. No stir of air was there;
* ~~Not so much life as what an eagle's wing~~ ~~a young vulture's~~
~~Would spread upon a field of green ear'd corn:~~
But where the dead leaf fell, there did it rest
A Stream went voiceless by, still deadened more
By reason of his fallen divinity
~~Shading across it~~
Spreading a shade: the Naiad mid her reeds
Press'd her cold finger closer to her lips.
Along the margin sand large footmarks went
No further than to where his feet had stay'd, sodden
And slept ~~without~~ there since ~~a motion: since that time~~ upon the ~~[illegible]~~ ground
His old right hand lay nerveless ~~on the ground~~ ~~dead & unfirm~~ listless, dead
Unsceptred; and his ~~white brow'd~~ ~~ancient~~ realmless eyes were clos'd;
While his ~~bowed~~ bow'd head seem'd listening to the Earth
~~His~~ His Ancient Mother for some comfort yet.
Thus the old Eagle drowsy with ~~his~~ ~~grief~~ great ~~woes~~ grief
Sat moulting his weak Plumage never more
To be restored or soar against the Sun,
While his three Sons upon Olympus stood—

* Not so much life as on a Summer's day
Robs not at all the dandelion's fleece

OPENING LINES OF KEATS'S MS. OF 'HYPERION'

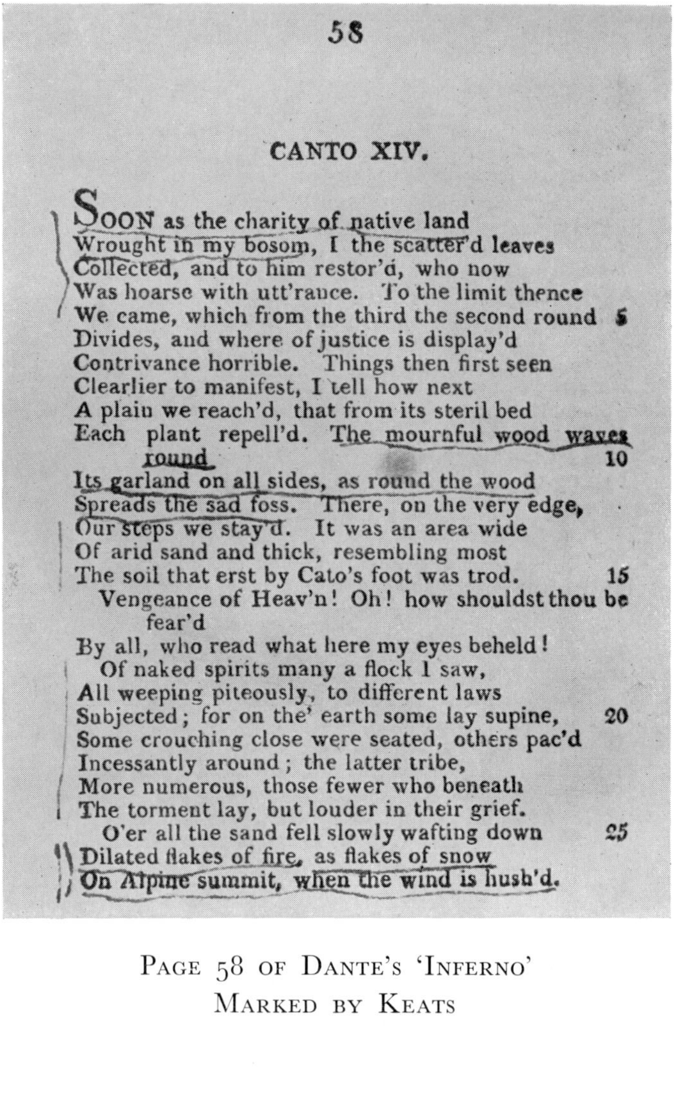

58

CANTO XIV.

SOON as the charity of native land
Wrought in my bosom, I the scatter'd leaves
Collected, and to him restor'd, who now
Was hoarse with utt'rance. To the limit thence
We came, which from the third the second round 5
Divides, and where of justice is display'd
Contrivance horrible. Things then first seen
Clearlier to manifest, I tell how next
A plain we reach'd, that from its steril bed
Each plant repell'd. The mournful wood waves
round 10
Its garland on all sides, as round the wood
Spreads the sad foss. There, on the very edge,
Our steps we stay'd. It was an area wide
Of arid sand and thick, resembling most
The soil that erst by Cato's foot was trod. 15
Vengeance of Heav'n! Oh! how shouldst thou be
fear'd
By all, who read what here my eyes beheld!
Of naked spirits many a flock I saw,
All weeping piteously, to different laws
Subjected; for on the' earth some lay supine, 20
Some crouching close were seated, others pac'd
Incessantly around; the latter tribe,
More numerous, those fewer who beneath
The torment lay, but louder in their grief.
O'er all the sand fell slowly wafting down 25
Dilated flakes of fire, as flakes of snow
On Alpine summit, when the wind is hush'd.

PAGE 58 OF DANTE'S 'INFERNO'
MARKED BY KEATS

By all, who read what here my eyes beheld!
Of naked spirits many a flock I saw,
All weeping piteously, to different laws
Subjected; for on the' earth some lay supine,
Some crouching close were seated, others pac'd
Incessantly around; the latter tribe,
More numerous, those fewer who beneath
The torment lay, but louder in their grief.
O'er all the sand fell slowly wafting down
Dilated flakes of fire, as flakes of snow
On Alpine summit, when the wind is hush'd.

To see how closely the vale, the forest, the margins and the sand of Keats resemble those of which he had read in Dante, it is necessary to notice some expressions used in his first draft of *Hyperion*, and different from the published version of the poem. To begin with, Keats's first draft shows a muddled and crossed-out attempt at line 7 of his poem:

Like Clouds that whose bosoms thundrous bosoms

which suggests that the opening lines of Canto xiv were in his mind. Far more strikingly, his manuscript of line 16 of *Hyperion* reads

No further than to where his feet had *stay'd*,

"Stay'd" and not "stray'd" was what Keats intended and wrote, and thus exactly echoed this peculiar use of the word in Cary's "Our steps we stay'd". That this is so was proved by the alteration that Keats made just a year later, when he was incorporating some of these lines into his new and even more fragmentary version of the epic, *The Fall of Hyperion—A Dream*. In this he changed the word "stayed" to "rested". It is clear from this that he meant "stayed" in the sense of "rested" or "stopped" —in the Italian, "fermammo"—and that "strayed" was imported into the poem against his intentions. In fact, it was probably done by his publishers without his consent, as were many alterations in the 1820 Poems, including the introductory note to *Hyperion* itself, which Keats repudiated.

At all events, his use of this distinctive word makes it certain that this part of the *Inferno* formed a great part of Keats's preparation for the opening of his own great poem. The first version of another line, which follows this, adds to the certainty. Keats had somewhat of a struggle before he arrived at the final version of the lines

Upon the sodden ground
His old right hand lay nerveless, listless, dead,

and for "listless, dead" his manuscript at one time read "dead, supine". This exactly matches the description in Dante of those who have been violent against God, "on the earth some lay supine" in Cary's words. One cannot leave this whole passage without commenting how the lines describing the falling sand impressed Keats--

Dilated flakes of fire, as flakes of snow
On Alpine summit, when the wind is hush'd.

This simile, underlined in the text and double-lined down the margin, evidently made him determined to find a matching image of equal beauty for his own poem. Before he arrived at his own lovely

Not so much life as on a summer's day
Robs not one light seed from the feather'd grass,

he had at first written

a young vulture's
Not so much life as what an eagles wing
Would spread upon a field of green ear'd corn

Not fully content with this, he turned back when he had completed Book I of *Hyperion* to substitute the couplet

Not so much life as on a summer's day
Robs not at all the dandelion's fleece

which was in its turn to be superseded by the final version. The care which Keats took over this is in part some reflection of his own delight at Dante's image.

Some of his other markings in this canto bear closely on his own poem. The description of Capaneus as

> Yon huge spirit, that, as it seems, heeds not
> The burning, but lies writhen in proud scorn,

which he underlined, seems to have passed into the unheeded and giant form of Saturn. When in *Hyperion* Thea appears, and approaching this huge form, which

> seem'd list'ning to the Earth,
> His ancient mother, for some comfort yet.

touches "his wide shoulders", it is a clear reminiscence of the lines again double-marked by Keats, describing the Old Man of Crete—

> An ancient form there stands and huge, that turns
> His shoulders towards Damiata,

and, in fact, the lines immediately before this in the canto describe how Rhea, Saturn's wife, had concealed the birth of Jove:

> It was the spot which Rhea, Saturn's spouse,
> Chose for the secret cradle of her son;
> And better to conceal him, drown'd in shouts
> His infant cries.

The opening of *Hyperion*, then, shows abundantly that Keats had prepared for his own epic by reading Dante's, and that Canto xiv in particular had formed the basis for the opening passages of Keats's great poem. After some fifty lines, however, quite another influence begins to be felt in the dialogue between Saturn and Thea. This is Shakespeare's *King Lear*, which we know Keats was re-reading in the first week of October 1818 as he continued his own poem with the dying Tom at his side. Yet while turning to this fresh inspiration, he caught some echoes from the last of his marked cantos in this section of the *Inferno*, the touching and tender Canto xv. This describes the meeting between Dante and his former instructor Brunetto

Latini, and is full of a deep sympathy between the two men, which combined, in Keats's mind, with the sympathy between Cordelia and the awakened Lear. Brunetto is condemned to walk the burning sand as an offender against Nature. Dante, walking the "margin-sand", keeps as close to him as he can—

> I dar'd not from the path descend to tread
> On equal ground with him, but held my head
> Bent down as one who walks in reverent guise.

Keats did not mark these lines, but they are echoed in Thea's approach to Saturn

> after bending low
> With reverence, though to one who knew it not.

Brunetto and Dante converse, as Thea and Saturn do; Keats double-marked Dante's loving apostrophe to Brunetto as

> The dear, benign, paternal image, such
> As thine was, when so lately thou didst teach me
> The way for man to win eternity:

Saturn, bewailing to Thea his lost influence as father of gods and men, cries

> I am smother'd up
> And buried from all godlike exercise
> Of influence benign on planets pale,
> And admonitions to the winds and seas,
> Of peaceful sway above man's harvesting,

and both the words and the tone of voice are very close to Dante's.

After this canto, there is a gap of six unmarked cantos covering twenty-six pages. We know, however, that Keats quoted from Canto xvii, and it is likely that he read on. Without his markings it is impossible to be certain, but there seem to be signs that he took up his reading in some of these cantos when he was completing Book I of his own poem, and embarking on Book II, that is, a month later, at the end of October 1818.

First, there are many parallels between the end of Canto xvii where Geryon

> Gathering the air up with retractile claws

sails down with Dante and Virgil on his back, and the end of *Hyperion* Book I, where Hyperion, urged by Coelus, descends to earth to find the fallen Titans. Coelus advises Hyperion to

> seize the arrow's barb
> Before the tense string murmur.

Geryon, his task done,

> forthwith
> Sprang forward like an arrow from the string.

Hyperion descended

> Then with a slow incline of his broad breast . . .
> And plung'd all noiseless into the deep night.

Geryon

> slowly sailing wheels
> His downward motion,

and Dante conceives new terror "at the steep plunge".

In the next canto, the eighteenth, the scene changes abruptly, just as it does in Book II of *Hyperion*. In the eighth circle of the *Inferno*,

> There is a place within the depths of hell
> Call'd Malebolge,

where the most severe torments take place. In *Hyperion*, where the fallen Titans were assembled,

> It was a place* where no insulting light
> Could glimmer on their tears;

but nevertheless a place of torment, rocky and "Stubborn'd with iron". This is not at all unlike Dante's Malebolge,

> all of rock dark-stain'd
> With hue ferruginous,

*Afterwards altered to "den".

and once again it is not unlikely that Keats has turned Cary's somewhat ponderous literal translation of "di color ferrigno" into his own individual, or at least semi-Shakespearean phrase. Although much of the Titan imagery comes from another source, Keats's re-reading of his letters to Tom about the Scottish mountains, the whole feeling of this place of despair is like that of Malebolge, and phrases such as

> along the grisly rock,
> Horn'd demons I beheld, with lashes huge,

seem to have provided some of the large-sized adjectives for Keats's impressive picture.

Keats did not mark these half-dozen cantos, and indeed probably gave up his reading of the *Inferno*, for reasons in his own life which struck him at this time with tremendous force, and which altered in some ways his whole habit of mind. He met two beautiful young women, Mrs. Isabella Jones and Fanny Brawne; his brother Tom died on December 1st; he himself moved into the house next to Dilke's, sharing it with the racy and worldly Charles Armitage Brown, whose literary interests leant to fantasy and drama. Under these various influences, and disappointment at the poor sale of his last book, he began to write a very different kind of poetry, and virtually gave up any systematic work on *Hyperion*. By the spring of 1819, he had only gone a short way into the third book of his poem, and in that fragmentary state the work remained until its publication in the summer of 1820, which has already been alluded to. The close study of the *Inferno* and the active composition of his own epic to match it both ceased. When the *Inferno* is next mentioned in Keats's letters, it is a re-reading to which he refers, and a very different set of his own poems with which he connects it.

IV

There is, in point of fact, one reference to Dante in Keats's letters which dates from early in 1819, but this is a semi-humorous one, and is not connected in any way with Keats's own poems. During the first fortnight in January of that year, Keats was greatly exercised in raising money for his friend

Benjamin Robert Haydon, the painter, whose financial affairs were in a state of perpetual chaos. Keats, who was legally entitled to some of the property of his dead brother Tom, had rashly promised Haydon a loan, but found the promise hard to keep, owing to difficulties placed in his way by Richard Abbey, the City tea-merchant, who administered the property. In a letter to Haydon, which Professor Rollins has dated as being written on January 12th, Keats wrote

> I shall have a little trouble in procuring the Money and a great ordeal to go through—No trouble indeed to any one else—or ordeal either. I mean I shall have to go to town some thrice, and stand in the Bank an hour or two—to me worse than any thing in Dante—.

This means little more than that Keats still had the *Inferno* in mind; the remark is typical of the slightly uneasy jocularity which he himself usually adopted about money matters, caused no doubt by the embarrassments which seem to have deliberately been put in his way by the disapproving Mr. Abbey.

Keats's next reference to the *Inferno* is, by contrast, direct and specific. It occurs just over three months later in a long journal letter to his brother George in America. These three months had been a space of severe and only partly-defined crisis for Keats, during which, according to Haydon who had a personal interest in his doings at this time, the poet "flew to dissipation as a relief". Part of the crisis of these months is certainly reflected in the earlier remarks in this passage of the letter.

> —The fifth canto of Dante pleases me more and more—it is that one in which he meets with Paulo and Francesca—I had passed many days in rather a low state of mind and in the midst of them I dreamt of being in that region of Hell. The dream was one of the most delightful enjoyments I ever had in my life—I floated about the whirling atmosphere as it is described with a beautiful figure to whose lips mine were joined at [*for* "as"] it seem'd for an age—and in the midst of all this cold and darkness I was warm—even flowery tree tops sprung up and we rested on them sometimes with the lightness of a cloud till the wind blew us away again—I tried a Sonnet upon it—there are fourteen lines but nothing of what I felt in it—O that I could dream it every night—

As Hermes once took to his feathers light
When lulled Argus, baffled, swoon'd and slept
So on a delphic reed my idle spright
So play'd, so charm'd, so conquer'd, so bereft
The dragon world of all its hundred eyes
And seeing it asleep so fled away:—
Not to pure Ida with its snow ~~clad~~ cold skies,
Nor unto Tempe where Jove grieved that day,
But to that second circle of sad hell,
Where in the gust, the whirlwind and the flaw
Of Rain and hailstones lovers need not tell
Their sorrows—Pale were the sweet lips I saw
Pale were the lips I kiss'd and fair the form
I floated with about that melancholy storm—

There is no doubt of the debt this sonnet owes to Canto v of the *Inferno*. Keats acknowledges it both here and in the first printed version, which appeared over a year later in the *Indicator* of June 28th, 1820. There is equally no doubt that the fascination of this episode, which led him to re-read it at this time, was also connected with circumstances in his own life. The section of the letter where he describes the dream and quotes the sonnet is dated April 16th, and the poem had in all probability been composed a few days before. On April 3rd, Dilke had moved out of the house next door to Keats, and Fanny Brawne, with her mother, brother and sister, had moved in. Her closeness brought matters to a head, and this poem celebrates their love as much as that of Paolo and Francesa.

It is notable that the poem is not by any means entirely inspired by Canto v, nor by the *Inferno* only, and that this was evidently therefore a personal re-reading, and not the close and deliberate "study" in which he had indulged in preparation for *Hyperion*. His particular "study" at this time was the works of Dryden, whose couplets he turned to good account two months later in his own *Lamia*. The first strong echo of Dryden's style in his own writing occurs in the light-hearted couplets of the *Extempore*, which he had scribbled in the same letter on the previous night, April 15th. Here, the whole of the octave of the sonnet is based on Book One of Ovid's Metamorphoses in Dryden's well-known translation, and echoes closely his telling of the story of Hermes and Argus.

It is, of course, only the sestet of the sonnet that catches the spirit and the words of Canto v, the second circle of the Carnal Lovers, where they float in the whirlwind, in Cary's translation, "as it is described",

> The stormy blast of hell
> With restless fury drives the spirits on
> Whirl'd round and dash'd amain with sore annoy.

Here too, in the sestet of the sonnet, Keats has strayed out of the second circle, and read on into Canto vi and the third circle of the Gluttons, guarded by Cerberus who perhaps thus turned his mind to the image of Argus. The second circle of the lovers is merely windy and stormy; it is the third circle, described at the beginning of Canto vi, that is both cold and wet.

> In the third circle I arrive, of show'rs
> Ceaseless, accursed, heavy and cold, unchang'd
> For ever, both in kind and in degree.
> Large hail, discolour'd water, sleety flaw. . . .

Keats's reading has plunged his vision further into Hell than he may have intended.

In all this, not even in this re-reading did Keats in any way mark the text of these cantos. This seems astonishing, considering their influence on him, and it can only be supposed that it was some part of Keats's system not to mark a book except at a first reading. That he was re-reading in this same volume of the *Inferno* is proved by the fact that this volume contains what is undoubtedly his first draft of the sonnet. On the inside of the back cover, he wrote in ink a trial opening:

> Full in the midst of bloomless hours my spright soul
> Seeing one night the dragon world asleep
> Arose.

Here, for a time, inspiration failed, and he perhaps turned to read Dryden, for it is in pencil, and in a less hurried hand, that the key words, which were to be the springboard for the sonnet, are added to the third line—"like Hermes". Keats now had the image which was to dominate the octave of the sonnet; a glance told him, too, that he had begun by spacing the lines too widely on the tiny rectangle. He turned back to the end fly-leaf, and wrote, beginning high up on the top of the page, and once more in ink, the version beginning

As Hermes once took to his feathers light

It is lucky that this is not the only version of the sonnet, for it is written in such haste of composition, and, necessarily, cramped into such a tiny space, that many words are nearly illegible, and strange transpositions take place—for example, the rhyming word "flaw" has to be put at the beginning of the next line, and the word "pale" makes its second appearance as "Plae". The whole manuscript has the air of swift and immediate composition.

Nor was this the only poem in manuscript to be influenced by these cantos and this translation of the *Inferno* at this time. About a week later, on April 21st, and in the same letter to George Keats, there appears the first draft of the famous *La Belle Dame Sans Merci*. Many threads may have spun together in the making of this magical poem, and even if all were to be traced, the work would still remain a miracle. Yet there is clearly some connection between the sonnet's

Pale were the sweet lips I saw
Pale were the lips I kiss'd and fair the form

and the lyric's two most evocative stanzas, which in their first draft read:

I saw pale Kings and Princes too
Pale warriors death pale were they all
They cried La belle dame sans merci
Thee hath in thrall.

I saw their starv'd lips in the gloam
All ~~tremble~~
gaped
With horrid warning / wide ~~agape~~
And I awoke and found me here
On the cold hill's side.

The connection is that both owe a great deal to Canto v of the *Inferno*, and to Francesca's story beginning

> "Love, that in gentle heart is quickly learnt,
> Entangled him by that fair form,

It was the most famous lines of that story that so influenced Keats, as they have done everyone who reads them:

> One day
> For our delight we read of Lancelot,
> How him love thrall'd. Alone we were, and no
> Suspicion near us. Ofttimes by that reading
> Our eyes were drawn together, and the hue
> Fled from our alter'd cheek. But at one point
> Alone we fell. When of that smile we read,
> The wished smile, so rapturously kiss'd
> By one so deep in love, then he, who ne'er
> From me shall separate, at once my lips
> All trembling kiss'd.

Cary's translation of this supreme passage may seem pedestrian, but it has its points. One of these is the way in which the blank verse is varied and broken up so as to achieve something of the flowing and lyric quality of the original *terza rima*. In this passage, by what must have been a special effort, he does this most successfully through a large number of run-on lines, and by the abruptly stopped half-lines of four syllables each:

> How him love thrall'd.
> Alone we fell.
> All trembling kiss'd.

Now, the striking and beautiful short line, which ends each stanza of *La Belle Dame*, has always been attributed to quite different areas of Keats's reading, to William Browne, the Elizabethan, with his "Let no bird sing" and Wordsworth with his "Her eye was wild". Both these phrases are indeed echoed in early stanzas of *La Belle Dame*; but the most probable unconscious reason for Keats's mind to adopt this four-syllable line in the rhyme-scheme of the whole poem, and thus give it its particular character, is not any poem that he may have read at some other time, but this passage in the *Inferno* which he is known actually to have been reading at this one time in his life. This attribution becomes almost a certainty when "How him love thrall'd", with its inversion of pronoun and verb, is repeated by "Thee hath in thrall" or, in later versions, "Hath thee in thrall", of *La Belle Dame.* The final proof is Keats's cancelled "All tremble" as he realised that what he was writing had an echo, which, though he probably could not place it, came from the "All trembling kiss'd" of the canto which he had so recently read and admired for the second time.*

It seems clear that what has been called "the metrical secret" of *La Belle Dame*, as well as much of its feeling, comes from this canto which, though unmarked by Keats, coloured his reading and thought in April 1819. As a postscript, it may be noticed that he at least allowed his eye to stray at this time to a passage which he had already marked with emphasis in Canto xiii. This is the description in the Wood of the Suicides of Pier delle Vigne, the minister of the Emperor Frederick II, who, until the year 1247 when he was suddenly disgraced, enjoyed the closest confidence of his master. As Pier tells Dante in the passage underlined by Keats

> I it was who held
> Both keys to Frederick's heart, and turn'd the wards,
> Opening and shutting with a skill so sweet,

Once more in the same journal letter to George, Keats includes some sonnets he has recently written. One of these is the experimental sonnet *To Sleep*, whose last line but one is

> Turn the key deftly in the oiled wards,

but in whose original draft, lines 9 and 10 read

> Then shut the hushed casket of my soul
> And turn the key round in the oiled wards

That this phrase was a favourite with Keats just at this time is shown by the way he repeated it in the *Extempore* of April 15th:

*Many of these points were noted by J. L. Lowes in a letter to the *Times Literary Supplement*, May 3rd, 1934, p. 322. He omitted to notice, however, the key point of the resemblance between Cary's half-lines and the short lines of *La Belle Dame*.

And touch'd the wards, the Door full courteously
Opened—

while even the arrangement of these light-hearted lines shows a certain connection with Canto xiii of the *Inferno*. Just after the line quoted, Keats breaks off, writes in mock-epic style

End of Canto xii

and opens the next section of his comic fable

Canto the xiii

These lines, however, show in their turn that Keats's re-reading of Dante during this April was only spasmodic and desultory, and that there was no attempt to take it up as before in serious study. The main reason is that he had finally dropped his own first version of *Hyperion*, for which he had first studied the *Inferno*. Richard Woodhouse, on April 20th, began a copy of the *Hyperion* fragment from Keats's MS., which was to all intents and purposes unchanged, and certainly not added to, when Woodhouse gave it to the press for publication a year later. The *Extempore*, as has been said, is the first evidence of Keats's intensive study of Dryden, which bore its chief fruit in the first part of *Lamia*, written at Shanklin in the summer of 1819, and the second part of the same poem, written in the autumn at Winchester. It is not until Winchester that the *Inferno* is once more mentioned in Keats's letters and taken up again in his reading and composition.

V

Keats moved to Winchester on August 12th, 1819, and stayed there for about eight weeks. He had come from a stay of six and a half weeks at Shanklin in the Isle of Wight, where he had written Part I of *Lamia*, four out of the five acts of his tragedy *Otho the Great*, and had been considering a new and ambitious attempt at a fresh version of *Hyperion*. It was probably the latter consideration that caused him to recommence his reading of the *Inferno*, and to make his third set of markings in the volume.

The evidence that he was reading the *Inferno* while at Winchester is the briefest and most laconic that we have. Writing once more to his brother George on September 21st, Keats remarks:

> In the course of a few months I shall be as good an Italian Scholar as I am a french one. I am reading Ariosto at present: not managing more than six or eight stanzas at a time. When I have done this language so as to be able to read it tolerably well—I shall set myself to get complete in latin, and there my learning must stop. I do not think of venturing upon Greek. I would not go even so far if I were not persuaded of the power the knowle[d]ge of any language gives one—the fact is I like to be acquainted with foreign languages. It is besides a nice way of filling up intervals &c Also the reading of Dante in well worth the while. And in latin there is a fund of curious literature of the middle ages. The Works of many great Men—Aretine and Sanazarius and Machievell.

Only the single sentence mentions Dante, though his slip of the pen—"in" for "is"—suggests that the word "Inferno" occupied his mind. The fact that Keats was learning Italian has led to a theory that he was now reading the *Divine Comedy* in the original. There is no evidence for this, and much to the contrary. Keats, on his own statement, was only able to manage six or eight stanzas of Ariosto at a time, and was unable to read the language even "tolerably well". It is most unlikely that he could yet master the complexities of Dante's Italian. No copy of the *Divine Comedy* in the original was found among Keats's books at his death, whereas there was certainly an Italian edition of Ariosto.

Moreover, his own works at this time show time and again the strongest possible connection with Cary's translation, and one small general point may at once be noted. At Winchester, Keats wrote five very varied poetic works—*Otho the Great*, Act V, the fragment of *King Stephen, a tragedy*, *Lamia*, Part II, the *Ode to Autumn* and the new *The Fall of Hyperion—A Dream*. In the first three works, as well as imagery common to all five, Keats is fond of using the distinctive and rather odd exclamation "Certes". This is the somewhat archaic expression Cary always uses to translate the characteristic Italian adjective "certo", which has always proved a well-known stumbling-block to English translators. That Keats was reading his third set of marked cantos (xxii to xxvii) may also be deduced from his letters. Two days later (September 23rd) he wrote to Brown on one of his favourite subjects, that imaginary evils are always worse than real ones.

> Real grievances are displacers of passion. The imaginary nail a man down for a sufferer, as on a cross;

This vivid image is also a very curious one. In speaking of crucifixion, it is natural to imagine the sufferer being nailed *up* and hanging, rather than fixed to the ground. In Canto xxiii of the *Inferno*, however, Dante finds among the Hypocrites who are punished there the figure of Caiaphas

> Fixed to a cross with three stakes in the ground;

so that the other Hypocrites may tread upon him as they pass. Keats underlined the words describing Caiaphas's agony—"ruffling with deep sighs his beard"—and his reading of this passage must be the origin of his own striking expression.

It is natural then to look to the beginning of Keats's stay at Winchester for the beginning of his third attentive marking of the *Inferno*. When he arrived, Keats had still an act of *Otho the Great* to complete. This he polished off within a week, and immediately began upon another tragedy, *King Stephen*, in which he hoped to write a part of manly action worthy of Edmund Kean. The play opens with three short battle-scenes in which Stephen defies his enemies single-handed, in an atmosphere of warlike bustle and excitement which constitutes some of Keats's finest dramatic writing. The first passage of the section of the *Inferno* which Keats now began to mark is the opening of Canto xxii. Dante and Virgil are escorted by a squad of ten armed demons beside a lake of boiling pitch, where lie those who have made an illegal traffic in public offices. Dante uses military metaphor, partly as a satire on the sinister company in which he finds himself marching.

It hath been heretofore my chance to see
Horsemen with martial order shifting camp,
To onset sallying, or in muster rang'd,
Or in retreat sometimes outstretch'd for flight:
Light-armed squadrons and fleet foragers
Scouring thy plains, Arezzo! have I seen
And clashing tournaments, and tilting jousts,
Now with the sound of trumpets, now of bells,
Tabors, or signals made from castled heights,
And with inventions multiform, our own,
Or introduc'd from foreign land; but ne'er
To such a strange recorder I beheld,
In evolution moving, horse nor foot,
Nor ship, that tack'd by sign from land or star.
  With the ten demons on our way we went;
Ah fearful company! but in the church
With saints, with gluttons at the tavern's mess.
  Still earnest on the pitch I gaz'd, to mark
All things whate'er the chasm contain'd, and those
Who burn'd within. As dolphins, that, in sign
To mariners, heave high their arched backs,
That thence forewarn'd they may advise to save
Their threaten'd vessel; so, at intervals,
To ease the pain his back some sinner show'd,
Then hid more nimbly than the lightning glance.

Keats drew a line down the margin of nearly all this passage, and he has matched it in the military energy of the poetry of his own play. Stephen, hemmed in, boasts that he will only yield "to some twenty squadrons". He is described not as a man,

But a fierce demon, 'nointed safe from wounds,
And misbaptized with a Christian name.

Moreover, Keats has taken the word "nimbly" as a special attribute for his hero. It is said that he makes his attacks "with a nimble savageness", and again, in his enemies' dialogue:

Gloucester. Did no one take him at a vantage then?
Second Knight. Three then with tiger leap upon him flew,
Whom, with his sword swift-drawn and
nimbly held,
He stung away again. . . .

This matches an incident later in Canto xxii. The demons haul out of the pitch a sinner who comes from Navarre. Circled by the fiends, the sinner yet manages to escape in spite of the threats of one of his enemies:

> "Quit we the vantage ground, and let
> The bank be as a shield; that we may see
> If singly thou prevail against us all."
> Now, reader, of new sport expect to hear!
> They each one turn'd his eyes to the' other shore,
> He first, who was the hardest to persuade.
> The spirit of Navarre chose well his time,
> Planted his feet on land, and at one leap
> Escaping disappointed their resolve.
> Them quick resentment stung, . . .

Keats's markings occur a few lines after this passage, but both in particular words, and in incident, it has a great likeness to the vivid dialogue of his own tragedy.

King Stephen, however, was abandoned with only four short scenes written. Keats had read in the journals that Kean was going on an American tour, and there would be no point in offering the play to him. Keats was also short of money, and it was high time he wrote the second part of *Lamia*. He did this in the last week of August and the first days of September. It required a special kind of "study" to catch the atmosphere of classical Greece for the poem, and this he found in John Potter's *Archæologia Græca*, of which he made extensive use. Even so, it is probable that he read on for at least one more canto of the *Inferno* at this time. Canto xxiii, that of the Hypocrites, begins with lines that Keats marked:

> In silence and in solitude we went,
> One first, the other following his steps,

while, though the lines are unmarked by Keats, Dante exclaims later on the same page:

> Already I perceiv'd my hair stand all
> On end with terror, and look'd eager back.

These two pairs of lines combined in Keats's mind to assist the dramatic introduction of the scene of horror at the end of the poem:

> A deadly silence step by step increased,
> Until it seem'd a horrid presence there,
> And not a man but felt the terror in his hair.

There is also just a possibility that the terrifying line marked by Keats in Canto xxv

> He ey'd the serpent, and the serpent him.

had its influence on this final scene of the poem, where the philosopher Apollonius fixes his relentless eyes on the serpent Lamia.

It is in fact in these next two cantos, xxiv and xxv, of the thieves tormented by and turned into serpents, that Keats's reading intensifies and his markings increase. He had now finished *Lamia*; he felt at the top of his writing form, and he was undistracted by the companionship of Charles Brown, who took himself off for three weeks. In these circumstances, his mind was free for his fresh project, a completely new start on the epic of *Hyperion* in an original and more individual way.

That way, he evidently decided, was to model its construction more closely on that of the *Inferno* itself. It was to be "A Dream", just as the *Divine Comedy* was "A Vision". Instead of the story being seen objectively, it was to be a subjective experience of Keats himself, and thus to become, as with Dante, far more of a personal allegory. Keats was to relate it in his own person, and, like Dante, to have a guide, not indeed a fellow-poet such as Virgil, but a mysterious female figure, the priestess Moneta. The first 180 lines, written early in September, tell of his meeting with Moneta. Keats partakes of an outdoor feast of fruit and wine. He swoons and awakes to find himself at the foot of gigantic steps leading to an altar tended by a veiled prophetess. He is warned that he must ascend the steps before she burns some "gummed leaves". After a terrible struggle, in which he is near to death, he succeeds. Like Dante, he has known

> What 'tis to die and live again before
> Thy fated hour.

Like Dante too, he engages in philosophic argument with the priestess who is henceforth to be his guide.

Since Keats was copying so closely the scheme of allegory adopted by Dante, he was naturally at pains to make the vision or dream specially his own, and not to import into it any direct incident or expression from the *Inferno*. It is therefore only in broad and impressive images and outlines that he owes any direct debt to his reading. In Canto xxiv, Dante follows Virgil in a terrible climb out of the den of the Hypocrites in which he suffers, as Keats does, an almost complete exhaustion. He then arrives among the Thieves, whom he first sees pierced by serpents and dissolved to dust, exactly as Keats's fate had been foretold, if he did not reach the altar before the leaves were burnt. The strange image of these "gummed leaves" burning has its parallel in the tremendous picture of Canto xxv, where men are described as taking on the form and nature of the serpents that seize them.

> Then, as they both had been of burning wax,
> Each melted into other, mingling hues,
> That which was either now was seen no more.
> Thus up the shrinking paper, ere it burns,
> A brown tint glides, not turning yet to black,
> And the clean white expires.

Keats marked all this long passage, and underlined in particular the wonderful image of the last three lines. There can be little doubt that his own haunting vision owes something to Dante's here.

At this point, a sudden and perhaps disastrous break occurred in Keats's composition. Forced to go to London for five days to try and raise money for George, he returned to Winchester in a restless state. On September 19th, in partly-restored calm, he wrote the serene *Ode to Autumn*. Although almost a poetic version of his own walks by the river as described in his letters, this ode has been shown to have a close literary affinity with a poem to Autumn by Chatterton, whom Keats actually mentions in connection with it. It has never before been noticed, however, how close it is to one of the most beautiful passages in the whole of the *Inferno*.

There is no doubt how deeply Keats was impressed by this passage, for he marked it with a double line down the margin.

It occurs near the beginning of the next canto he read, Canto xxvi, and comes like a calm respite in the midst of horrors.

As in that season when the sun least veils
His face that lightens all, what time the fly
Gives way to the shrill gnat, the peasant then
Upon some cliff reclin'd, beneath him sees
Fire-flies innumerous spangling o'er the vale,
Vineyard or tilth where his day-labour lies:

As well as its cadence and feeling, so like that of Keats's

Season of mists and mellow fruitfulness,

this perfect image has its echoes in the "small gnats" of the Ode, and the vines, which somewhat strangely twine their Mediterranean growth round the thatch-eves of Keats's poem. The reclining peasant watching the fruit of his labours has his counterpart in the beautifully personified figure of Autumn in the Ode.

How much more of *The Fall of Hyperion—A Dream* Keats continued to write at Winchester is uncertain. He himself announced that he was giving up both versions of the epic, in his disturbed state, on September 21st, but there is evidence that he continued to tinker with the new version later in the autumn. Once more, it is isolated and striking images that he takes from his marked reading in the *Inferno*. Later in Canto xxvi, where Dante meets the Givers of Evil Counsel, now turned into flames, Keats seems to have been deeply impressed by the image of the double flame, representing Ulysses and Diomed, who planned the Wooden Horse of Troy. Keats marked three occurrences of this image—

who is in yon fire, that comes
So parted at the summit,

To pause here, till the horned flame arrive.

Of the old flame forthwith the greater horn
Began to roll,

and unconsciously he adapted its strange picture to the altar flame of his own mysterious priestess—

> . . . 'Holy Power,'
> Cried I, approaching near the horned shrine,
>
> . . . then again
> I look'd upon the altar and its horns
> Whiten'd with ashes and its lang'rous flame,

Another strong image occurs in Canto xxvii, the next and the last to be marked by Keats, where Dante is addressed by another Evil Counsellor, Count Guido da Montefeltro.

> Long as this spirit mov'd the bones and pulp
> My mother gave me, less my deeds bespake
> The nature of the lion than the fox.
> All ways of winding sublety I knew,

Keats, now conducted by Moneta to the scene of his own first *Hyperion*, sees Saturn, and hears the words of the fallen giant. Among the many strange lines he adds to his former version at this point, he describes how Saturn's speech echoes in the oaks

> And to the windings in the foxes' holes.

There are also many minor verbal likenesses between these marked cantos and Keats's vocabulary in this "Dream", notably the use of "tribe" for "species" and "ken" for "view".

There is no evidence that Keats ever read the last seven cantos of the *Inferno*. They are unmarked, and, according to Mr. Rabinowitz, the pages look as though they were unread. There are one or two hints, in the sequence of *The Fall of Hyperion*, which perhaps suggest that he may have glanced at these remaining cantos and adopted some of the images from them. He was now largely repeating passages from the beginning of the first *Hyperion* with some alterations, not always for the better, and the addition of some new and often strange images, which are worth consideration. The very remarkable new description of Saturn near the end of Keats's Canto One

> Like a vast giant seen by men at sea
> To grow pale from the waves at dull midnight

may have some relation to the description of the giants that line the shore of the lake at the beginning of Dante's Canto xxxi. Moneta's address to Keats at the beginning of his second canto

'Mortal, that thou mayest understand aright,

has much of the tone of Dante's address to the reader at the commencement of his own next canto, No. xxxii, while another new description of Saturn just before Keats breaks off his epic, this time for ever, as "rous'd from icy trance", may reflect Dante's entrance into the ninth, last, and frozen circle of Hell in this same canto.

It is, however, an alteration which Keats made in quite a different poem that suggests he may at least have looked at the end of the *Inferno*, even if he did not, in the stress of this time of his life, read continuously or carefully. During this profoundly unhappy time for him, the last three months of 1819, he attempted every now and again to prepare his completed poems for the volume which was to come out in 1820. We hear of one such attempt in the third week of December. Among these were some alterations to *The Eve of St. Agnes*, which he showed to George, who appeared in England early in the New Year on a flying visit which complicated Keats's problems still further. Most of these alterations were silently removed by the publishers before the poem came out, and in general it is as well that they were. One particularly awkward and curious change by Keats is in Stanza xiv, where the old servant makes the perfectly satisfactory remark in the course of a speech to the hero, Porphyro,

'To venture so: it fills me with amaze
'To see thee, Porphyro!

Keats substituted for this the puzzling expression:

'To venture so about these thorny ways
A tempting Be'lzebub

It looks as if his eye had lighted on the last canto of the *Inferno*; there Dante and Virgil climb with difficulty out of Hell over the monstrous body of "Belzebub" in Cary's translation (in the

Italian, "Belzebu"), and it is worth noting that Milton, by contrast, always spells and makes "Beëlzebub" a four-syllable word.

Yet no reading of unmarked passages can be completely guaranteed, unless it is vouched for in Keats's own letters. This applies still more to the theories which have been raised, my own among them, about Keats's reading in the *Purgatorio* and the *Paradiso*. There is no evidence that he ever opened the volumes containing these poems. Perhaps the likenesses which have been adduced between these two sections of the *Divine Comedy* and *The Fall of Hyperion* arise from the simple fact that, as we have observed, this poem, unlike *Hyperion* itself, was conceived and intended to be constructed on the same basic plan as Dante's poem. The coincidences of the veiled priestess, for example, who resembles various veiled figures, including Beatrice, in both the *Purgatorio* and *Paradiso*, may be explained simply by the fact that Keats was now following, in his way, the basic plan of the older poet.

This may be summed up by saying that Keats was deeply indebted to his reading in this little volume, in the first place for the atmosphere and imagery of much in his *Hyperion*, and secondly for the ground-pattern and some of the more striking imagery in his *The Fall of Hyperion*. On his way, his reading of the volume, for the purpose of his own two epic attempts, made its mark on some of his finest sonnets, on *La Belle Dame Sans Merci*, on the fragment of *King Stephen*, and on some small portion of *Lamia* Part II and the *Ode to Autumn*.

This is not to say that the *Inferno* was the sole influence on these poems, for Keats drew his inspiration from many sources, and, in his reading, frequently kept several books on the go at the same time. It is interesting to note that whenever he is reading Dante, he is also apparently reading Milton—except, of course, on the Scottish excursion, and even then his letters are full of Miltonic quotations. Both the *Inferno* and *Paradise Lost* probably fulfilled for him those moods when he felt the need for something of epic stature. There are signs that he regarded Milton's poem as the greater work; in his notes he commends the scheme of *Paradise Lost* for not being "grotesque", which may reflect his opinion of some of the incidents in the *Inferno*. He also noted his preference for the more sustained tenderness of Milton in comparison with the "brief pathos" of Dante. Yet for all these opinions, which may in part be due to the less successful sides of Cary's translation, it is clear that this little volume provided a strong element of poetic nourishment for Keats during and beyond his own greatest year of composition. The simplest demonstration of this lies in the complete list of his markings in the *Inferno*, reproduced at the end of this book, and the relevant passages of Keats's own poetry which are added to them.* With these, side by side, we can make some study of how Keats went to work; without claiming to explain the mystery, we can at least draw closer to it.

*Appendices A and B.

3

MORE ABOUT MRS. JONES

To Mary Moorman

ONE would like to know more about Mrs. Isabella Jones, most especially for the sake of the poems with which she is connected. *The Eve of St. Agnes*, perhaps the finest narrative poem in the language, was written by Keats, according to the respectable evidence of Richard Woodhouse, "on the suggestion" of this lady. It is tolerably certain that its beautiful though fragmentary companion-piece, *The Eve of St. Mark*, was written on her suggestion also, and that her rooms, which Keats visited frequently in the winter of 1818–19, are portrayed in the description of the room of the heroine, Bertha. There is also strong evidence that Isabella is the "Isabel" of the lively lyric *Hush, hush!*, written at about this time, and, strongest of all, that the first version of Keats's sonnet *Bright Star* coincides with the reappearance in his life of this enigmatic and beautiful young woman.

An enigma—the word is Keats's—she remains. Her mysterious injunction that her friendship with the poet should be concealed from the friends they had in common seems to have been well kept. It is, however, among the friends she possessed outside the poet's immediate circle that, as I have suggested elsewhere, some clue to her personality and position may lie. These friends were of a very different age, type and background from those of the poet, and it may be conjectured that, by commands such as that which she laid on Keats himself, she was able to keep these two worlds tactfully and comfortably apart.

This second world seems to have had as its centre—according to his own letters and those of Keats's publishers—an elderly gentleman named O'Callaghan. O'Callaghan was in the habit of recuperating from his illnesses "of body and of mind" at or near Hastings, where Keats had first met and, according to his own account, carried on a warm flirtation with Isabella Jones in the early summer of 1817. This flirtation seems, as we shall see, to be connected with yet another poem by Keats, just as, it may be thought, O'Callaghan himself is "the jealous old bald-pate" of the lively lines to "Isabel" in *Hush, hush!* At all events, O'Callaghan was known to Keats's publishers as a special friend of Isabella Jones, and one who, for her sake and in spite of his choleric temper, was not to be offended.

Who, then, was Mr. O'Callaghan? The question has been complicated for us by his own execrable handwriting. Admittedly, it is that of a very elderly and often excitable gentleman, but very little as illegible can ever have been written. In general, one hieroglyph does for nearly all consonants, and another for nearly all vowels. As i's are seldom dotted, and t's hardly ever crossed, the confusion is complete. Only painfully can the sense of ordinary words be made out, and proper names naturally are a problem all on their own. Among these, the Christian name in his own signature provides a severe test, and for a long time I have been able to read it only as "Donal", an Irish form of "Daniel". Close comparison with other similar words in his handwriting, however, now reveals that what appeared to be an "l" is in reality an uncrossed "t". The name therefore appears as "Donat", and one which gives us far more chance of identifying Isabella Jones's friend among the numerous tribe of eighteenth-century O'Callaghans.

These were largely sprung from a certain Cornelius O'Callaghan of Shanbally Castle, County Tipperary. Just before his death in 1740, this gentleman proudly compiled a list of his numerous progeny, including seven sons. To one of these, Thomas, were born two boys, Cornelius on January 7th, 1741, and the younger, Donagh or Donat, named after an uncle, on October 17th, 1743. This Cornelius was destined to raise the family to distinction, and to connect it with English politics. He married Frances Ponsonby, of the great Whig family of that name, and after, apparently, some protracted debates behind the scenes in Whig circles, he himself was created Baron Lismore on June 27th, 1785. During this time the career of his younger brother is obscure, but there is no doubt that he is

Isabella Jones's Donat O'Callaghan. In his letters, he displays a close familiarity with people in just those Whig circles of which Baron Lismore was a member. Moreover, there is another piece of evidence to show that Isabella Jones was on close terms with these Lismore O'Callaghans. In May 1819, she went to Tunbridge Wells for her health. There she would have found Frances, Dowager Lady Lismore, by then a widow, who died there on May 25th, 1827; but what connects her even more surely with the Whig family of Lismore is that her letter from that place, written to Keats's publisher, was franked for her by yet another member of the family, Lieutenant-Colonel James O'Callaghan, M.P.

James O'Callaghan is spoken of in various contemporary works as having a close family connection with the Lismores, and therefore with the Ponsonby and other Whig families. He was Member in the Whig interest for the rotten-borough of Tregony in Cornwall in 1806, 1807, 1818 and 1820. In the first of these years, the second Baron Lismore, created Viscount Lismore in that year, represented the neighbouring town of Listowel for the Whigs. James, though a much older man, seems to have been confused by some people with the Viscount's younger brother, Robert William, who was also at that time a Lieutenant-Colonel, afterwards rising to eminence as a General in the Peninsular War. James was born in 1748, and was therefore five years younger than Donat O'Callaghan, of whom he was a first cousin. It is typical of the times that the privilege of franking, confined to Members of Parliament, should be used by James O'Callaghan to send free a letter from Isabella Jones, his cousin Donat's friend, and, incidentally, Keats's.

James O'Callaghan had a slight connection with literature rather less indirect than that. Perhaps on the eighteenth-century principle that Members for rotten-boroughs lived as far away as possible from their constituency, he had made his home at Heighington in County Durham, where his friend and patron Lord Darlington was a large coal-owner. Lord Darlington was a nephew of Margaret, sister of the first Lord Lonsdale, and hence James O'Callaghan, though a Whig, obtained the entrée to the High Tory society of the Lonsdales, and was invited to stay with them at Lowther Castle. He is the "O'Callaghan who knows Lowther well" of Creevey's letters, a notable tribute to his standing with both political parties. It was at Lowther Castle that he met Wordsworth, a favoured Tory guest, and it was in an album kept by James O'Callaghan, which still exists, that Wordsworth in 1824 inscribed a sonnet. He is mentioned in a letter* of the previous year from the poet to Lord Lonsdale, in which it is implied that O'Callaghan, although grey-haired, was an extremely vigorous character.

This, indeed, may throw some light on the association of the still young and beautiful Mrs. Jones with the two septuagenarian Irishmen. The O'Callaghan stock appears to have been exceptionally long-lived and virile. Outliving his second wife Hannah who died in 1817, and a son Daniel, by an earlier marriage, who died in 1825, James O'Callaghan married in 1827, at the age of 79, Miss Margaret Simpson of Barnard Castle, who must have been considerably younger than himself, since her father was one of the executors of his Will. A similar liveliness and virility of expression pervades the letters of Donat O'Callaghan, who also must have been in his middle seventies at the time of his association with Isabella Jones. What certainly appears from all this is that Isabella Jones moved in circles of some distinction. The brother of Baron Lismore, and so brother-in-law of a member of the distinguished house of Ponsonby, Donat O'Callaghan could claim—as indeed he hints in one letter—high political connections, both through them and through his cousin James the M.P. Isabella may well have had tactical reasons for wanting to keep quiet her friendship with the young, ardent and extremely radical Keats, and her secrecy about their association becomes less of an enigma.

It is likely too that these political connections were not merely a matter of social prestige with her, but had perhaps a definite pecuniary value. Her rooms, described by Keats, were well-furnished and expensive. Those which he saw have since disappeared, but those into which she soon afterwards moved, at the then 57 Lamb's Conduit Street (now 49) still exist. One can see how spacious they were, and guess at their furnishings by the elaborate stuccoed ceilings which still remain. One of these represents a flying Cupid, with bent bow, while the other, by what can surely only be a coincidence, seems to represent the dawning of a sun-god, Hyperion or Apollo. Both, in their

* Communicated to me by Mary Moorman.

Seal Used by Isabella Jones

Hastings, from a Contemporary Print

rich symbolism, are much in the spirit of the handsome design with which Isabella sealed her letters—the sun sinking behind hills, with the motto "Je reviendrai". All this clearly had to be paid for, and it may well be thought that the O'Callaghans provided the money. Donat O'Callaghan was evidently not only well-connected but well-to-do. We hear of him ordering from Taylor & Hessey, a specially, expensively-bound volume of Horace, intended, it seems, as a gift for the 15th Earl of Rothes, then a schoolboy at Eton.

It is likely that one can trace a gift for Isabella which seems to have been paid for out of the O'Callaghan pocket. In 1819, her miniature, by the fashionable painter A. E. Chalon, was hung in the Royal Academy exhibition at Somerset House. She wrote to John Taylor, asking him to go and see it. Six years later, another miniature by Chalon appeared in the Royal Academy exhibition catalogue as being of "Master J. W. D. O'Callaghan". This is practically certain to be a misprint for George William Douglass O'Callaghan, who had just joined the Navy as a midshipman. This boy, who afterwards rose to the rank of Admiral with a record of distinguished service in the China Seas, seems to have been the illegitimate son of another brother of the Viscount and the General, George O'Callaghan, who incidentally was a contemporary at Eton of Richard Woodhouse. The boy's first two names were derived from his father and from his uncle the General; it may be guessed that Douglass, not an O'Callaghan name, was that of his unknown mother. At all events, the O'Callaghans employed Chalon to paint him, and in view of the close connection between them and Mrs. Jones, it seems more than a coincidence that the same artist should have painted her. It is probable that her miniature was commissioned by one of the O'Callaghans. Yet whatever her connection with the O'Callaghans, the problem of who precisely she was still remains. The only Mrs. Isabella Jones who appears in any documents of the time, public or private, was the young widow of a naval lieutenant, drawing a pension from the Navy Board. She, however, became insane in 1813. Keats's Isabella still deserves the title that Sir Sidney Colvin gave her—"the mysterious Mrs. Jones".

A final problem about her, which has proved easier of

solution, is whether she had in her possession any poems of Keats, other than those mentioned which are associated with her name. C. L. Finney remarked that a copy of the following lyric by Keats has against it the shorthand note "From Miss Reynolds and Mrs. Jones".

You say you love; but with a voice
  Chaster than a nun's, who singeth
The soft Vespers to herself
  While the chime-bell ringeth—
    O love me truly!

You say you love; but with a smile
  Cold as sunrise in September,
As you were Saint Cupid's nun,
  And kept his weeks of Ember.
    O love me truly!

You say you love—but then your lips
  Coral tinted teach no blisses,
More than coral in the sea—
  They never pout for kisses—
    O love me truly!

You say you love; but then your hand
  No soft squeeze for squeeze returneth,
It is like a statue's, dead,—
  While mine to passion burneth—
    O love me truly!

O breathe a word or two of fire!
  Smile, as if those words should burn me,
Squeeze as lovers should—O kiss
  And in thy heart inurn me!
    O love me truly!

There are three manuscript copies of this poem in existence, none of them by Keats. One is in a book belonging to his friend J. H. Reynolds (though not in Reynolds's handwriting), one is in the book of transcripts by Richard Woodhouse at Harvard, and the third, apparently in the hand of Keats's publisher John Taylor, is in the Morgan Library. This last has a point of difference from the other two. The first line of Stanza II reads

You say you love; but then you smile

which seems to give a touch more of reality to the slightly formal little lyric. This alteration is copied, in pencil, by Woodhouse over the line in his transcript; it is in pencil too, and apparently at the same time, that Woodhouse has added the shorthand note "and Mrs. Jones" to the original note of "From Miss Reynolds", which appears at the end of his transcript.

A reasonable explanation of all this may be found. Isabella Jones possessed, perhaps written by Keats in some album, the version of the poem with the line

You say you love; but then you smile

Sometime, probably after Keats's death, when Taylor and she were exchanging letters about the poet, Taylor copied her version, and communicated it to Woodhouse. Woodhouse had meanwhile obtained a version from J. H. Reynolds, which Keats had written out for one of Reynolds's sisters. When Woodhouse received Isabella Jones's version from Taylor, he noted the variant wording above the line in his own copy, and added her name to his shorthand note on the source for the poem. At all events, this seems certainly to mean that Keats had given the same lyric, with one minor difference, to two young women. Which came first depends on whether one regards the altered line in Isabella Jones's copy as an improvement or not. It is not perhaps unknown for poets to make the same poem do for two ladies; and Keats, a very human poet and a very young man, was not less likely than others to do this. The little poem has never been dated before, but in style and imagery it recalls other lyrics which he wrote during the year 1817, when his mind was mainly occupied with the major work of *Endymion*. It may well be associated with Keats's first meeting with Isabella Jones, in the early summer of that year, when, in the poet's own words, he "warmed with her . . . and kissed her". Perhaps, on looking back, he reflected that she had not been as warm as he might have hoped; "she has always been an enigma to me."

In the meantime, can any more be gathered of the intellectual interests which she and Keats had in common, those "matters of knowledge and taste" in which he hoped to be, as he said, "of service to her"? Apart from the evidence that she suggested one of his greatest poems, and was the probable recipient of several of his minor works, the longest document which records her "knowledge and taste" is the lively letter she wrote to John Taylor on the subject of Severn's account of Keats's last days in Rome.* Since this was published, many people have objected to the merciless criticism to which she subjects Severn in its pages; they forget, perhaps, that she is only echoing the more kindly comment of the doctor who attended Keats:

> He has a friend with him who seems very attentive to him but between you & I is not the best suited for his companion, but I suppose poor fellow he had no choice.

At all events, her attack on Severn is important for revealing, between the lines, at least one piece of reading which she and Keats had in common. This is Laurence Sterne's *Tristram Shandy*; quotations and passages in the style of this work colour many of the livelier pages of Keats's own letters, and similar Shandean echoes are to be found here in hers. In fact, it seems as if Keats and she had what he called his "rhodomontade" style in common. The most obvious moment occurs where she sums up her disgust at the sentimental and moralising style which Severn had adopted:

> Of all the cants, in this canting world the cant of sentiment is the most disgusting and I never saw better specimens than these letters afford——

This, doubtless suggested by the fact that Severn was an artist and her satire on his painting a few lines before, is a clear though perhaps unconscious recollection of Sterne's outburst on art-criticism:

> Grant me patience, just Heaven!—Of all the cants which are canted in this canting world,—though the cant of the hypocrites may be the worst,—the cant of criticism is the most tormenting!

Now Keats himself was familiar with this passage; this can be guessed from a letter which he had written to Severn himself in

* First printed in full in my *John Keats: The Living Year*, pp. 231-3.

March 1819, also on the subject of art. Speaking of Severn's request to hang the miniature he had painted of Keats in that year's Royal Academy exhibition at Somerset House, the poet wrote that "Even a large picture is lost in that canting place". The miniature was in fact hung, and its number in the catalogue, 940, makes it practically certain that it appeared in the same room as Isabella Jones's miniature by A. E. Chalon, which was No. 895. Thus we may conclude that Keats and Isabella Jones not only had their Shandean reading in common, but that they both borrowed from Sterne a vigorous style in dealing with affectation of any sort, particularly that of art. The whole of Isabella Jones's letter, indeed, may strike one as a "rhodomontade" very much in the manner of Keats himself, though Keats, with his warm sympathy for the weaker side of man's nature, would seldom have used his gift for amusing invective on a human subject. This difference between the high-spirited and pungent temper of both of them may have insured that their relationship, in spite of common interests, could not last for long, even without Isabella's enigmatic prohibition.

4

"BRIGHT STAR"

To J. R. MacGillivray

I

THE date of composition of Keats's *Bright Star* sonnet has always intrigued critics, ever since it was realised that its familiar sub-title, "Keats's Last Sonnet", was a false one, and that an earlier draft existed. Before putting forward reasons to suppose that this draft can be dated to an exact day, it may be as well to quote this early version:

Bright star! would I were stedfast as thou art!
Not in lone splendour hung amid the night;
Not watching, with eternal lids apart,
Like Nature's devout sleepless Eremite,
The morning waters at their priestlike task
Of pure ablution round earth's human shores;
Or, gazing on the new soft fallen mask
Of snow upon the mountains and the moors:—
No;—yet still stedfast, still unchangeable,
Cheek-pillow'd on my Love's white ripening breast,
To touch, for ever, its warm sink and swell,
Awake, for ever, in a sweet unrest;
To hear, to feel her tender-taken breath,
Half-passionless, and so swoon on to death.

The grounds on which critics have dated this version have always appeared somewhat arbitrary, though most have agreed with Charles Brown, Keats's friend, in assigning it to the year 1819. Brown, however, was not always accurate—certainly not as accurate as Richard Woodhouse—in dating Keats's work; without Woodhouse's supporting evidence, all his dates must be treated with reserve. Sir Sidney Colvin, on apparently no more evidence than lines 7 and 8 of the sonnet, dated it confidently as being composed on the night of February 24th/25th, 1819, when snow fell in London. Miss Amy Lowell, in her life of Keats, produced more plausible reasons for the night of April 15th/16th. Following Professor Rusk, she observed how closely the opening lines of the sonnet resemble Keats's description of Lake Windermere:

> There are many disfigurements to this Lake—not in the way of land or water. No; the two views we have had of it are of the most noble tenderness—they can never fade away—they make one forget the divisions of life; age, youth, poverty and riches; and refine one's sensual vision into a sort of north star which can never cease to be open lidded and stedfast over the wonders of the great Power.

This description occurs in Keats's letter to his brother Tom, which, Miss Lowell argued, Keats had in his hands and re-read on the evening of April 15th. She did not observe, however, that Keats had already forwarded this letter to his other brother, George, in America, five and a half months before. There have been various other conjectures, mostly connected with the weather Keats was experiencing or the places where he was staying. None, however, appears to have caused such comment as my own dating of the sonnet to the last week in October 1818. It is in response to such comments, notably those of Mr. Middleton Murry, that I should like here to produce more evidence that the sonnet was not only composed at this time, but very probably at one particular and exact date —the night of October 26th/27th, 1818.*

This involves repeating, to some extent but with a great deal of additional evidence, the double argument that I have used before. Put very simply, it is this:

(1) That the sonnet shows close affinity not only with the letter to Tom (which has been a commonplace with many critics before myself) but with Shakespeare's play of *Troilus and Cressida*.

(2) That there is one date, and only one, on which everything that Keats writes, in his letters to relatives and friends, is packed with quotations, half-quotations, and ideas both

* See note p. 174.

from the letter to Tom and from his own heavily-marked copy of the play.

Mr. Murry has tried to dispose of the first part of the argument by saying that he cannot see the resemblances; of the second, by saying that Keats is full of quotations from Shakespeare and that isolated single quotations from *Troilus and Cressida* occur in four other letters of Keats. If, however, the double affinity of the sonnet to both the letter to Tom and the play is clear, and if, on a certain date, not merely single quotations, but a round dozen quotations from letter and play together are packed into everything else that Keats was writing —then, I think, the probability that he also wrote the sonnet on this exact date becomes, in default of any better suggestion, overwhelming. That is what I shall attempt to show.

It must be remembered that in the last week of October 1818, Keats himself says that he had got out the letter to Tom, together with one or two others, first with the idea of making a copy and then in order to send it to his brother George, which he did on October 31st. Even without this hint it is impossible not to see the likenesses between the sonnet and the portion of the letter which has been quoted. This has often been noticed. It has not been noticed that a part of the sonnet which has sometimes been quoted as a weakness—the second half of the eighth line—is also taken from the letter—"the mountains and the moors". Keats's amazed delight at first seeing the "mountains", as he calls them, from above Bowness is commented on specially by Brown, his companion. When he came to write to Tom he could not stop mentioning them, and used the word half a dozen times in the letter—"an amazing partiality for mountains" is one of his own descriptions of this state of mind. Nor is the word "moor" lacking in this recital; he mentions twice the name of the place from which they set out early that morning—End Moor. "The mountains and the moors", far from being a poetic afterthought, are directly taken over from this source of the poem's imagery.

As for the second source—Shakespeare's *Troilus and Cressida*—one must take particular care. Resemblances between the works of one poet and another are often largely a matter of the ear that hears them. There is also a common stock of poetic imagery upon which all poets draw. On the other hand, there are often cadences and turns, hardly definable but nevertheless real, which the sensitive listener can hear, but which argument is often hard put to it to demonstrate. One must steer a course between these two, bearing in mind the dictum that Keats himself marked in his copy of *Troilus and Cressida*:

> For pleasure and revenge
> Have ears more deaf than adders to the voice
> Of any true decision.

In other words, one must not start with any initial prejudice, to hear or not to hear.

One of the longest continuous passages that Keats marked in this play is the beginning of Act III, Scene II, where Pandarus is about to bring Cressida to Troilus. The feelings of Troilus as he waits are expressed in a way very like the final couplet of Keats's sonnet. Troilus anticipates the outcome of love's experience as overpowering

> death, I fear me;
> Swooning destruction;

while, for Keats, the pleasures of sense and touch will make him "swoon on to death". It is to be noted that, in this folio copy, Keats altered the text's "Sounding destruction" to "swooning" in his own hand. A few lines later, also marked by Keats, Pandarus describes Cressida

> She fetches her breath so short as a new-ta'en sparrow.

This also bears much relation, in feeling and cadence, to the "tender-taken breath" of the sonnet. In fact, the whole of the second half of the sonnet is specially Shakespearian, with its distinctive compound epithets—"tender-taken", "cheek-pillow'd", "soft-fallen". One of these seems to be an echo of a phrase of Pandarus which Keats marked in the scene immediately preceding (Act III, Scene I), where he addresses Helen:

> faire thoughts be your faire pillow

It is not, however, only the later part of the sonnet which seems to be related to Keats's marking of the play. The most beautiful and striking image

> The morning waters at their priestlike task
> Of pure ablution round earth's human shores

is typical of Keats, and the lines are among the finest he ever wrote. It does not detract from them to notice how Shakespearian they are, nor how their basic idea is found expressed in a very similar way in another marked passage in this play. For Ulysses, in his famous speech on "Degree" (Act I, Scene III) has exactly the same idea. He, however, imagines the chaos which would ensue if the power that rules both waters and shores were taken away:

> The bounded waters
> Should lift their bosoms higher than the shores
> And make a soppe of all this solid Globe:

Keats has followed Shakespeare's vision, and universalised the "beautiful water—shores" of Lake Windermere, from the letter to Tom, into the larger image of the waters and shores of the whole world.

These are verbal instances of how the sonnet echoes the play. There is, besides, what, to use Keats's words in the letter to Tom, may be called the "countenance or intellectual tone" which sonnet and play have in common. It is not, of course, rare for Keats to catch cadences from Shakespeare: Dr. Caroline Spurgeon has given a long and convincing list of the Shakespearian echoes which are to be found in *Endymion*. I think that anyone reading *Troilus and Cressida* together with the *Bright Star* sonnet will be struck by these resemblances in tone —the great, universal, generalised images of the octave of the sonnet paralleled by Ulysses's philosophical speeches in the play, and the personal passion of the sestet finding its counterpart in the emotional experiences of Troilus himself.

So much to establish that the sonnet shows this double affinity, both with Keats's letter to Tom and with *Troilus and Cressida*: now to turn to what Keats was writing on the night of October 26th/27th, 1818.

II

He was writing two letters, which one need not scruple to quote in full, since they are among his finest and most characteristic utterances in prose. The first is his famous reply to Richard Woodhouse's letter of October 21st. In it, Keats sets out his own idea of the poetic character and his plans for his own poetic future.

My Dear Woodhouse,

Your Letter gave me a great satisfaction; more on account of its friendliness, than any relish of that matter in it which is accounted so acceptable in the 'genus irritabile'. The best answer I can give you is in a clerk-like manner to make some observations on two principle points, which seem to point like indices into the midst of the whole pro and con, about genius, and views and atchievements and ambition and cœtera. 1st. As to the poetical Character itself (I mean that sort of which, if I am any thing, I am a Member; that sort distinguished from the wordsworthian or egotistical sublime; which is a thing per se and stands alone) it is not itself—it has no self—it is every thing and nothing—It has no character—it enjoys light and shade; it lives in gusto, be it foul or fair, high or low, rich or poor, mean or elevated—It has as much delight in conceiving an Iago as an Imogen. What shocks the virtuous philosopher, delights the camelion Poet. It does no harm from its relish of the dark side of things any more than from its taste for the bright one; because they both end in speculation. A Poet is the most unpoetical of any thing in existence; because he has no Identity—he is continually in for—and filling some other Body—The Sun, the Moon, the Sea and Men and Women who are creatures of impulse are poetical and have about them an unchangeable attribute—the poet has none; no identity—he is certainly the most unpoetical of all God's Creatures. If then he has no self, and if I am a Poet, where is the Wonder that I should say I would write no more? Might I not at that very instant have been cogitating on the Characters of Saturn and Ops? It is a wretched thing to confess; but is a very fact that not one word I ever utter can be taken for granted as an opinion growing out of my identical nature—how can it, when I have no nature? When I am in a room with People if I ever am free from speculating on creations of my own brain, then not myself goes home to myself: but the identity of every one in the room begins to [*for* so] to press upon me that I am in a very little time an[ni]hilated—not only among Men; it would be the same in a Nursery of children: I know not whether I make myself wholly understood: I hope enough so to let you see that no dependence is to be placed on what I said that day.

In the second place I will speak of my views, and of the life I purpose to myself. I am ambitious of doing the world some good: if I should be spared that may be the work of maturer years—in the interval I will assay to reach to as high a summit in Poetry as the nerve bestowed upon me will suffer. The faint conceptions I have of Poems to come brings the blood frequently into my forehead. All I hope is that I may not lose all interest in human affairs—that the solitary indifference I feel for applause even from the finest Spirits, will not blunt any acuteness of vision I may have. I do not think it will—I feel assured I should write from the mere yearning and fondness I have for the Beautiful even if my night's labours should be burnt every morning, and no eye ever shine upon them. But even now I am perhaps not speaking from myself: but from some character in whose soul I now live. I am sure however that this next sentence is from myself. I feel your anxiety, good opinion and friendliness in the highest degree, and am

Your's most sincerely,

JOHN KEATS.

This letter is undated but postmarked HAMPSTEAD 27 OC 1818. It bears, I think, evidence of having been composed late at night—the phrase about "my night's labours", for instance—and this was a favourite time for letter-writing with Keats. The second letter was written to his brother George in America. It is in fact the latter part of a long journal letter despatched on the last day of October 1818, and so evidently written in the last week of that month. Phrases in it, which repeat almost word for word those in the letter to Woodhouse, make it equally evident that it was written on the same night. It was again a habit with Keats to do his letter-writing in bursts of energy, writing, when he did, to several people at once, and to repeat whole phrases from one letter in another. There can be no doubt that these words to George, expanding the personal side of the letter to Woodhouse and echoing all its ideas, were written within a very short time of the latter.

> Notwithstand[ing]your Happiness and your recommendation I hope I shall never marry. Though the most beautiful Creature were waiting for me at the end of a Journey or a Walk; though the carpet were of Silk, the Curtains of the morning Clouds; the chairs and Sofa stuffed with Cygnet's down; the food Manna, the wine beyond Claret, the window opening on Winander mere, I should not feel—or rather my Happiness would not be so fine, as my Solitude is sublime. Then instead of what I have described, there is a Sublimity to welcome me home. The roaring of the wind is my wife and the Stars through the window pane are my Children. The mighty abstract Idea I have of Beauty in all things stifles the more divided and minute domestic happiness—an amiable wife and sweet Children I contemplate as a part of that Beauty —but I must have a thousand of those beautiful particles to fill up my heart. I feel more and more every day, as my imagination strengthens, that I do not live in this world alone but in a thousand worlds. No sooner am I alone than shapes of epic greatness are stationed around me, and serve my Spirit the office which is equivalent to a King's body guard—then 'Tragedy with scepter'd pall, comes sweeping by." According to my state of mind I am with Achilles shouting in the Trenches, or with Theocritus in the Vales of Sicily. Or I throw my whole being into Triolus and repeating those lines, 'I wander like a lost Soul upon the stygian Banks staying for waftage", I melt into the air with a voluptuousness so delicate that I am content to be alone. These things combined with the opinion I have of the generallity of women—who appear to me as children to whom I would rather give a Sugar Plum than my time, form a barrier against Matrimony which I rejoice in. I have written this that you might see I have my share of the highest pleasures and that though I may choose to pass my days alone I shall be no Solitary. You see there is nothing spleenical in all this. The only thing that can ever effect me personally for more than one short passing day, is any doubt about my powers for poetry—I

> seldom have any, and I look with hope to the nighing time when I shall have none. I am as happy as a Man can be—that is in myself I should be happy if Tom was well, and I knew you were passing pleasant days—Then I should be most enviable—with the yearning Passion I have for the beautiful, connected and made one with the ambition of my intellect. Th[i]nk of my pleasure in Solitude, in comparison of my commerce with the world—there I am a child—there they do not know me not even my most intimate acquaintance—I give into their feelings as though I were refraining from irritating a little child—Some think me middling, others silly, others foolish—every one thinks he sees my weak side against my will, when in truth it is with my will—I am content to be thought all this because I have in my own breast so great a resource. This is one great reason why they like me so; because they can all show to advantage in a room, and eclipese from a certain tact one who is reckoned to be a good Poet—I hope I am not here playing tricks 'to make the angels weep'; I think not: for I have not the least contempt for my species; and though it may sound paradoxical: my greatest elevations of Soul leave me every time more humbled—

These two letters, allowing for the more intimate feelings which Keats always expressed to his own brother, are entirely akin in ideas and phraseology, the letter to George being an expansion of the second part of the letter to Woodhouse, and therefore probably written immediately after it with hardly any pause. Phrases such as "the mere yearning and fondness I have for the Beautiful" in the first letter are repeated almost exactly by "the yearning Passion I have for the beautiful" in the second. What these letters also have in common is that, in phraseology and ideas, they both are full of quotation, half-quotation, and reminiscence from the letter to Tom and Keats's marked passages from *Troilus and Cressida*.

These actual verbal likenesses may best be seen in the form of a tabulated list, which I have added as an appendix*; it is sufficient to note them briefly before passing to what is perhaps even more significant, the likenesses of ideas and thought. To begin with the Woodhouse letter—in one of its earliest phrases, Keats speaks of "two principle points, which seem to point like

* Appendix C.

indices into the midst of the whole pro and con". This is a reminder of Nestor's speech in *Troilus and Cressida*, Act I, Scene III, and the section, marked by Keats, beginning

> And in such Indexes, although small prickes
> To their subsequent Volumes

More striking are the resemblances to be found in almost the next phrase, where Keats describes one kind of poetic genius as

> the wordsworthian or egotistical sublime; which is a thing per se and stands alone

This phrase is compounded from the letter to Tom and his reading in *Troilus and Cressida*. Wordsworth, as described in the letter, is "Lord Wordsworth" who likes having his house pointed out, while in *Troilus and Cressida*, Act I, Scene II, Ajax is described exactly in these words, which Keats marked:

> They say he is a very man per se and stands alone

Keats then goes on to discuss his own kind of poetical character

> it is not itself—it has no self . . . not myself goes home to myself:

This is an echo, and a very important one, of the philosophic discussion between Ulysses and Achilles in Act III, Scene III of the play:

> For speculation turnes not to it selfe,
> Till it hath trauail'd, and is married there
> Where it may see it selfe

The next and very important parallel occurs between Keats's remarks on his own poetic ambitions and another speech of Ulysses, this time in Act I. This last is on a page where Keats not only marked many lines, but added a note in his own handwriting on Shakespeare's own poetic character. The reminiscence of this in Keats's plans for his own poetic future is striking. In the letter to Woodhouse, he says of himself:

> I will assay to reach to as high a summit in Poetry as the nerve bestowed upon me will suffer. The faint conceptions I have of Poems to come brings the blood frequently into my forehead.

On the heavily-marked page of the play, Keats underlined Ulysses's description of Agamemnon as "Nerve, and Bone of Greece". His MS. note on the same page, only a line or two away, describes the heights reached by Shakespeare, "his in(n)ate universality". It adds

> His plans of tasks to come were not of this world . . . how tremendous must have been his Conception of Ultimates.

Nor does the letter to Tom fail to contribute to Keats's description of his own poetic "ultimates". To Woodhouse he writes of "the solitary indifference I feel for applause even from the finest Spirits", while to Tom he had written of "that mass of beauty which is harvested from these grand materials, by the finest spirits".

The other letter written on the night of October 26th/27th, the portion of the journal letter to George Keats, exhibits the same number of close parallels with marked passages in the play and with the letter to Tom. His "chairs and Sofa stuffed with Cygnet's down" recall

> to whose soft seizure,
> The Cignets Downe is harsh.

of Act I, Scene I, of *Troilus and Cressida*. Immediately following this, "the Window opening on Winander mere" is taken from his experiences, retailed to Tom, of when he went to call on Wordsworth at Rydal Mount "along the border of Winandermere", for in his next letter to Tom, which was also in his hands on this night of October 26th/27th, he says of Wordsworth "his parlor window looks directly down Winandermere;" it is ironic that Keats's ideal view should be the one which Wordsworth actually owned.

When Keats speaks, in this letter as in the one to Woodhouse, of his poetic ambitions, he again echoes similar reflections, made four months earlier in the letter to Tom, and called forth by the grandeur of the lake and mountain scenery. To George he writes of "The mighty abstract Idea I have of Beauty in all things", while to Tom he had written of "the abstract endeavour of being able to add a mite to that mass of beauty". To George he exclaims "I feel . . . as my imagination strengthens, that I do not live in this world alone", recalling his remark to Tom, "I live in the eye; and my imagination, surpassed, is at rest——". Two final parts of the letter to George echo *Troilus and Cressida*. He exclaims "I wander, like a lost Soul upon the stygian Banks staying for waftage", misquoting but keeping the sense of the marked lines

> I stalke about her doore
> Like a strange soule upon the Stigian bankes
> Staying for waftage.

A few lines later, Keats's phrase "the generallity of women" echoes Shakespeare's "the general sex", which Keats marked in Troilus's disillusioned speech in Act V, Scene II.

These are verbal resemblances only, but there are a dozen of them, and some are startlingly exact, arguing a close reading of both play and letter at this time. What is also startling is a parallel of thought between Keats's philosophy at this time and a certain scene in *Troilus and Cressida*. This thought is not new in Keats. It is an extension of his doctrine of "Negative Capability", also applied to Shakespeare, in a letter to his brothers ten months earlier—the state of mind, in a great poet, in which "the sense of Beauty overcomes every other consideration, or rather obliterates all consideration". This is now developed, in the letter to Woodhouse, to the statement that "the poet has . . . no identity . . . no self". That the statement takes this turn is almost certainly due to a passage of dialogue that Keats had read, and partly marked, in *Troilus and Cressida*, Act III, Scene III.

This is the scene, just after the scene between hero and heroine, so heavily marked by Keats, in which the other Greek leaders pass by Achilles with studied indifference. Ulysses then approaches him, reading, or pretending to read, a book. Achilles asks him what he is reading, and these speeches ensue.

Ulysess: A strange fellow here
Writes me,
That man, how dearly ever parted,
How much in having, or without or in,
Cannot make boast to have that which he hath,
Nor feels not what he owes but by reflection;
As when his virtues shining upon others
Heat them, and they retort that heat again
To the first giver.

Achilles: This is not strange, Ulysses
The beauty that is borne here in the face
The bearer knows not, but commends itself
To others' eyes; nor doth the eye itself—
That most pure spirit of sense—behold itself,
Not going from itself; but eye to eye oppos'd
Salutes each other with each other's form;
For speculation turns not to itself
Till it hath travell'd and is mirror'd there
Where it may see itself. This is not strange at all.

Ulysses: I do not strain at the position,
It is familiar, but at the author's drift;
Who in his circumstance expressly proves
That no man is the lord of any thing—
Though in and of him there be much consisting—
Till he communicate his parts to others:
Nor doth he of himself know them for aught
Till he behold them form'd in the applause
Where they're extended; who, like an arch, reverberate
The voice again, or, like a gate of steel
Fronting the sun, receives and renders back
His figure and his heat.

In these speeches, Keats has only marked the last few lines of Achilles, and

who, like an arch, reverberate
The voice again,

from Ulysses, but it seems clear that their expression and philosophy have given the turn, which he himself gives, in this letter to Woodhouse, to his already-forming ideas about the nature of the poet. Indeed, he carries it further. Not only is the poet ignorant of himself and his gifts until he sees them reflected in others, but his own "identity" or personality is "annihilated" by others until "not myself goes home to myself" but only the creations of his art live. "Speculation", in Achilles's word, only sees itself when it has "travelled". "Speculation","—this time the word is Keats's—is the end of creative activity, into which the creator's own personality is so merged as to become unidentifiable. It is this thought that brings us back to the sonnet, *Bright Star*. For, in the letter to Woodhouse, the poet is the one person or thing who has nothing "unchangeable" about him. The sonnet is a reaction from the personal loneliness of that thought. In love, at least, let the poet be "unchangeable"—the word of the sonnet repeats the word of the letter to Woodhouse—be, for once, himself, with an "identity", like "The Sun, the Moon, the Sea and Men and Women", or, as he added in the sonnet, the star itself.

Thus, *Bright Star*, which has verbal affinities with both the letter to Tom and *Troilus and Cressida*, has a philosophic affinity, too, with the letters of October 26th/27th, 1818, which show so many echoes and parallels of these two sources. It is beyond the scope of this enquiry to speculate what made him compose it; but it does seem, as near as ever reasonable proof can draw to truth, that every piece of evidence available points to the sonnet being composed at this exact time. The critics who oppose such a conclusion have a reason for doing so; for there is some doubt whether Fanny Brawne, with whom the sonnet has traditionally been associated, had in fact met Keats by the end of October 1818. Apart from this biographical consideration, however, all the evidence from Keats's own reading and writing seems overwhelmingly to point to this one night in the last week of October 1818, when Keats, by the bedside of the dying Tom, sat composing, "obliged to write, and plunge into abstract images". His main work at this time was, of course, the first two books of the epic *Hyperion*. Further examination shows that there are noteworthy parallels between the end of *Hyperion* Book I and the beginning of *Hyperion* Book II on the one hand, and *Bright Star*, the letter to Tom, and *Troilus and Cressida* on the other: the word "passionless", cancelled in the draft of *Hyperion*, used in this version of the sonnet, is only one of these. Yet the main proof rests on the double source of the expression of the sonnet, and the double source of the quotations and ideas used in the two letters written on this identical night: in default of any more definite evidence, I hope I have shown that we should accept this proof. We may want the first version of *Bright Star* to have been inspired by Fanny Brawne; but this should not blind us to the many facts which point to the night of October 26th/27th, 1818, as the time at which Keats is most likely to have first drafted this much-debated poem.

5

TROILUS TO CRESSIDA

To J. Middleton Murry

KEATS wrote four poems to Fanny Brawne, none of which was published during his lifetime. Although one would not wish them unpublished, they are hardly Keats at his best. They are, perhaps, typical of those poems called forth by a particular occasion, which are of intense moment to the poet and his immediate circle, but which look strangely in the company of his more considered work. Not one, as a poem, is without severe flaws; on the other hand, all have flashes of Keats's strongest and most assured manner. All have a language, a feeling and a philosophy in common, and were clearly written within a very short time of one another, a fact which becomes evident when we consider them together in the probable order in which they were written.

LINES TO FANNY

What can I do to drive away
Remembrance from my eyes? for they have seen,
Aye, an hour ago, my brilliant Queen!
Touch has a memory. O say, love, say,
What can I do to kill it and be free
In my old liberty?
When every fair one that I saw was fair,
Enough to catch me in but half a snare,
Not keep me there:
When, howe'er poor or particolour'd things,
My muse had wings,
And ever ready was to take her course
Whither I bent her force,
Unintellectual, yet divine to me;—
Divine, I say!—What sea-bird o'er the sea
Is a philosopher the while he goes
Winging along where the great water throes?

How shall I do
To get anew
Those moulted feathers, and so mount once more
Above, above
The reach of fluttering Love,
And make him cower lowly while I soar?
Shall I gulp wine? No, that is vulgarism,
A heresy and schism,
Foisted into the canon law of love;—
No,—wine is only sweet to happy men;
More dismal cares
Seize on me unawares,—
Where shall I learn to get my peace again?
To banish thoughts of that most hateful land,
Dungeoner of my friends, that wicked strand
Where they were wreck'd and live a wrecked life;
That monstrous region, whose dull rivers pour,
Ever from their sordid urns unto the shore,
Unown'd of any weedy-haired gods;
Whose winds, all zephyrless, hold scourging rods,
Iced in the great lakes, to afflict mankind;
Whose rank-grown forests, frosted, black, and blind,
Would fright a Dryad; whose harsh herbag'd meads
Make lean and lank the starv'd ox while he feeds;
There (bad?) flowers have no scent, birds no sweet song,
And great unerring Nature once seems wrong.

O, for some sunny spell
To dissipate the shadows of this hell!
Say they are gone,—with the new dawning light
Steps forth my lady bright!
O, let me once more rest
My soul upon that dazzling breast!
Let once again these aching arms be plac'd,
The tender gaolers of thy waist!
And let me feel that warm breath here and there
To spread a rapture in my very hair,—
O, the sweetness of the pain!
Give me those lips again!
Enough! Enough! is it enough for me
To dream of thee!

Sonnet

The day is gone, and all its sweets are gone!
 Sweet voice, sweet lips, soft hand, and softer breast,

Warm breath, light whisper, tender semi-tone,
  Bright eyes, accomplish'd shape, and lang'rous waist!
Faded the flower and all its budded charms,
  Faded the sight of beauty from my eyes,
Faded the shape of beauty from my arms,
  Faded the voice, warmth, whiteness, paradise —
Vanish'd unseasonably at shut of eve,
  When the dusk holiday—or holinight
Of fragrant-curtain'd love begins to weave
  The woof of darkness thick, for hid delight;
But, as I've read love's missal through to-day,
He'll let me sleep, seeing I fast and pray.

Ode to Fanny

I

Physician Nature! let my spirit blood!
  O ease my heart of verse and let me rest;
Throw me upon thy Tripod, till the flood
  Of stifling numbers ebbs from my full breast.
A theme! a theme! great Nature! give a theme;
            Let me begin my dream.
I come—I see thee, as thou standest there,
Beckon me out into the wintry air.

II

Ah! dearest love, sweet home of all my fears,
  And hopes, and joys, and panting miseries,—
To-night, if I may guess, thy beauty wears
            A smile of such delight,
            As brilliant and as bright,
As when with ravished, aching, vassal eyes,
            Lost in soft amaze,
            I gaze, I gaze!

III

Who now, with greedy looks, eat up my feast?
  What stare outfaces now my silver moon!
Ah! keep that hand unravished at the least;
            Let, let, the amorous burn—
            But, pr'ythee, do not turn
The current of your heart from me so soon.
            O! save, in charity,
            The quickest pulse for me.

IV

Save it for me, sweet love! though music breathe
  Voluptuous visions into the warm air;
Though swimming through the dance's dangerous wreath,
        Be like an April day,
        Smiling and cold and gay,
A temperate lily, temperate as fair;
        Then, Heaven! there will be
        A warmer June for me.

V

Why, this—you'll say, my Fanny! is not true:
  Put your soft hand upon your snowy side,
Where the heart beats: confess—'tis nothing new—
        Must not a woman be
        A feather on the sea,
Sway'd to and fro by every wind and tide?
        Of as uncertain speed
        As blow-ball from the mead?

VI

I know it—and to know it is despair
  To one who loves you as I love, sweet Fanny!
Whose heart goes fluttering for you every where,
        Nor, when away you roam,
        Dare keep its wretched home,
Love, love alone, has pains severe and many:
        Then, loveliest! keep me free,
        From torturing jealousy.

VII

Ah! if you prize my subdued soul above
  The poor, the fading, brief, pride of an hour;
Let not profane my Holy See of love,
        Or with a rude hand break
        The sacramental cake:
Let none else touch the just new-budded flower;
        If not—may my eyes close,
        Love! on their lost repose.

SONNET

I cry your mercy—pity—love!—aye, love!
  Merciful love that tantalises not,
One-thoughted, never-wandering, guileless love,
  Unmask'd, and being seen—without a blot!
O! let me have thee whole,—all—all—be mine!
  That shape, that fairness, that sweet minor zest
Of love, your kiss,—those hands, those eyes divine,
  That warm, white, lucent, million-pleasured breast,—
Yourself—your soul—in pity give me all,
  Withhold no atom's atom or I die,
Or living on perhaps, your wretched thrall,
  Forget, in the mist of idle misery,
  Life's purposes,—the palate of my mind
Losing its gust, and my ambition blind!

When were they written? It is now generally thought that they date from October 1819 when, as Mr. Middleton Murry has convincingly pointed out, Keats's attachment to Fanny Brawne first ceased to be an "understanding" and took on the stature of a formal engagement. This is supported by the fact that the middle section of the first *Lines to Fanny* undoubtedly refers to the disastrous trading venture of Keats's brother George in America, which, at this time, obsessed the poet's mind almost as much as his jealous love for Fanny—"perplex me a great deal" is John's typical understatement in concealing the true state of George's affairs from their school-girl sister. Then again, the ideas and metaphors of the poems show close verbal affinity with part of Robert Burton's *The Anatomy of Melancholy*, which Keats was reading and quoting in his letters at this time, especially the later subsections "On Love-Melancholy" and, even more significantly, the early subsections "On Jealousy".

There is, however, another piece of evidence, unobserved till now, which dates the poems positively to this time. It does more than that. It provides some clue to the passionate and sometimes extravagant expression that pervades the poems: it shows something of what Keats was to himself in his own mind at this time. This evidence is contained in—or rather, added to—a letter written by Keats to Fanny Brawne from his temporary lodgings in College Street, Westminster, and post-marked 11 October 1819.

My sweet Girl,

I am living to day in yesterday: I was in a complete fa(s)cination all day. I feel myself at your mercy. Write me ever so few lines and tell you (*for* me) you will never for ever be less kind to me than yesterday—. You dazzled me. There is nothing in the world so bright and delicate. When Brown came out with that seemingly true story again(s)t me last night, I felt it would be death to me if you had ever believed it—though against any one else I could muster up my obstinacy. Before I knew Brown could disprove it I was for the moment miserable. When shall we pass a day alone? I have had a thousand kisses, for which with my whole soul I thank love—but if you should deny me the thousand and first—'twould put me to the proof how great a misery I could live through. If you should ever carry your threat yesterday into execution—believe me 'tis not my pride, my vanity or any petty passion would torment me—really 'twould hurt my heart—I could not bear it. I have seen Mrs Dilke this morning; she says she will come with me any fine day.

Ever yours,

John Keats

Ah hertè mine!

This letter, of course, contains many of the images that occur in the first *Lines to Fanny*—"bright", "dazzle", and so on—but it is the postscript that is the clue. If we enquire what was in Keats's mind when he scribbled the three words "Ah hertè mine", we may go some way towards seeing him as he saw himself.

The words themselves have never so far been identified, a curious omission when almost every other of the numerous quotations or, more often, misquotations in Keats's letters has been traced to its source. This is probably because Keats was fond of a kind of fake-mediæval language, connected partly with his reading of Chatterton, and tried his hand at it more than once in poetry and in prose. Editors may have assumed that this was a "Rowleyism", like those of Chatterton, on Keats's part. It is, however, a genuine quotation of a mediæval source, and, if one looks on a little further in Keats's letters, the clue is not far to seek. Keats that autumn had been reading Italian authors, in an attempt to learn that language; but in the middle of November he wrote to his publisher "I would rather read Chaucer than Ariosto". The words "Ah hertè mine" are from a certain part of Chaucer's most finished and impressive narrative poem, *Troilus and Criseyde*.

The part of the poem from which the words are taken is one of the most poignant in the whole long and tragic love-story. Criseyde, or Cressida, has been taken to rejoin her father in the Grecian camp. Troilus, her lover, remains besieged in Troy, having seen her taken away by the Greek Diomed, who already has begun to make advances to her. Troilus returns home, hurls himself down on his bed, and cries out frantically to himself in the four stanzas that follow:

Wher is myn owene lady lief and dere,
Where is hir whyte brost, wher is it, where?
Wher been hir armes and hir eyen clere,
That yesternight this tyme with me were?
Now may I wepe allone many a tere,
And graspe aboute I may, but in this place,
Save a pilowe, I finde nought t'enbrace.

How shal I do? Whan shal she com ayeyn?
I noot, allas! why leet ich hir to go?
As wolde god, ich hadde as tho be sleyn!
Oh herte myn, Criseyde, oh swete fo!
Oh lady myn, that I love and no mo!
To whom for ever-mo myn herte I dowe;
See how I deye, ye nil me not rescowe!

Who seeth yow now, my righte lodesterre?
Who sit right now or stant in your presence?
Who can conforten now your hertes werre?
Now I am gon, whom yeve ye audience?
Who speaketh for me right now in myn absence?
Allas, no wight; and that is al my care;
For wel wot I, as yvel as I ye fare.

How shulde I thus ten dayes ful endure,
Whan I the firste night have al this tene?
How shal she doon eek, sorwful creature?
For tendernesse, how shal she this sustene,
Switch wo for me? O pitous, pale, and grene
Shal been your fresshe wommanliche face
For langour, er ye torne un-to this place.

Before considering the relation between these stanzas and the four poems that Keats himself wrote, the inference of Keats's postscript to the letter is clearly shown by the continuation of the quotation, as it appears in Chaucer's second stanza. It is "Criseyde, oh swete fo", and it exactly describes Keats's complicated feelings at this time. For, it is evident, the formal engagement to Fanny Brawne did not at the time bring him happiness. It was an experience of acute conflict for him, accentuated, it would seem, by her behaviour. Out of the three letters he wrote to her this October, two, including the one quoted, speak of her uttering a "threat" to him, and the remaining letter contains the phrase "if you ever intend to be cruel to me as you say in jest now but perhaps may sometimes be in earnest". "Oh sweet foe" exactly describes what Keats felt about Fanny at this moment, and must be taken as implied by the postscript to the letter.

What is even more striking is the likeness between Keats's four poems and the four stanzas by Chaucer. From the first word, he borrows the whole cadence and language of the older poet. The rhetorical questions, the exclamations of these poems, so unlike the style in which Keats had just been writing —his last completed poem was the serene *Ode to Autumn*— become understandable when we see them side by side with the hysterical rhetoric that Chaucer gives to the sorely-driven Troilus. His cries of "Who", "What", "How" are especially paralleled in the two longer poems that Keats wrote, which borrow their whole tone most directly from Chaucer. The first *Lines to Fanny*, indeed, even introduce a slight awkwardness of speech in taking over an archaism straight from Troilus. The line "How shall I do", instead of "What shall I do", as Keats might normally have written, opens the second part of his first poem, precisely as it opens the second stanza of Chaucer's.

Where Keats seems to be speaking most with Chaucer's voice is in the *Ode to Fanny*. This is important, for it used to be thought that this ode was written much earlier in the relationship of Keats and Fanny, and bore some reference to the greater Odes of the spring and early summer of the year 1819. That it does not, but, on the contrary, sticks very closely in its whole tone and expression to Chaucer, is seen at a glance when one compares its third stanza with the third stanza of Troilus's complaint. During the past summer, while Keats had been absent from her, Fanny had formed the habit of going out to dances with military men, among whom her mother had some acquaintance. Keats addresses her and her partners at the ball in precisely the same way as Chaucer makes Troilus address Cressida as he sees her, in his imagination, with Diomed and the other warriors in the Greek camp. Exactly the same note of jealous possessiveness is there; the images are alike—"my righte lodesterre" of Troilus and "my silver moon" of Keats—but it is the whole tone and attitude of the lover in both passages that corresponds so closely. The manifestations of jealousy, in fact or in fiction, may follow a depressingly similar pattern: but there is more than such casual similarity about the way this is expressed. For the moment, Keats *is* Troilus. The two sonnets, though the resemblances are slighter, tell the same tale, and the passionate hysteria of the final sonnet finds its exact counterpart in Chaucer's hero.

If Keats was Troilus, Fanny, rightly or wrongly, in his fevered imagination, was Cressida. This we know. When, in February of the following year, ill-health brought a period of calm and a temporary cessation of these overwrought feelings, Keats wrote to her

> My greatest torment since I have known you has been the fear of you being a little inclined to the Cressid;

It is well known how intensely Keats read Shakespeare's play. The fact that, later in 1820, he quotes to Fanny some lines from it as applying to himself, has led to its being believed that he had Shakespeare's heroine and not Chaucer's in mind when he thought of her. Both may have been later present in his mind; but if, as seems likely, he was harking back to this terrible month of October, it would be Chaucer's Criseyde who had stepped in between his tortured vision and Fanny as she really was.

Most poets dramatise their lives. All are affected, though not always so much as Keats, by the appositeness of what they are reading to their own life's situation, and this, in turn, may affect, heighten, or falsify the situation itself. This is what seems to have happened here with Keats, "the chameleon poet". There is no reason to believe that Fanny was a Cressida, nor anything, in fact, other than a high-spirited playful young woman; there would be little point in seeking for a Diomed. On the other hand, Keats, for the time being, was Troilus, Chaucer's Troilus. The poems he wrote at this unhappy time are both the witness and the result of this passionate self-identification.

6

KEATS'S FATHER

To Dorothy Hewlett

I

WE know more of Shakespeare's father than we do of Keats's; there is a mystery about Keats's origins which no biographer has so far cleared up. Nor has the poet helped.

> Enchanted has it been the Lord knows where

is his sole and mysterious comment on the family name. Keats was only eight and a half when his father died in a riding-accident; but even then, such silence is strange.

Apart from the accident which caused his death in April 1804, the facts about Thomas Keats, the poet's father, can be counted on the fingers of one hand. He was thirty when he died, and was therefore born in early 1774 or late 1773. He came from the West Country, and, before he was twenty, became head ostler in the livery-stables of John Jennings, the Pavement, Moorgate. On October 29th, 1794, he married his master's daughter, Frances. He later moved to Craven Street, City Road, which was his home at the time of his death. Cowden Clarke, the son of Keats's schoolmaster, remembered the poet's father as a man of fine and energetic character. No other facts about him, or descriptions of him, exist. Cowden Clarke says that his fatal riding-accident occurred after a visit to his son at school at Enfield; the less reliable Richard Abbey, Keats's guardian, hints at a party and heavy drinking as contributing to the fatality.

Two obvious questions occur, among the many that must be aroused by these few facts. Why did Thomas Keats come to London, and where exactly did he come from? As it happens, a chance remark on both these topics may help us to trace, if not to a certainty, at least with some measure of probability, the answer to each.

First, why did the poet's father come to London? The clue, which may lead us some way in this direction, is provided by B. W. Procter ("Barry Cornwall"). Writing to Leigh Hunt, with a present of a brace of partridges, in 1858, Procter recounted a recent experience of his.

> I made the acquaintance, at Brighton, of a bookseller of the name of 'Keats.' I said 'Mr. Keats, you bear the name of a very fine poet'—'Yes, sir,' (he answered) 'I was a second cousin of Mr. Keats. I have more than once talked about him, with Mr. Leigh Hunt.' 'Well, I know Mr. Leigh Hunt very well and I know Mr. Keats the poet also.' 'Ah!—I am related also to Mr. Sheriff Keats——' 'I don't know him,' (I replied) 'but you may depend upon it that the poet was the greatest man. I advise you to stick to him.' Our friend proceeded—'I was in business in London—and Mr. Carlyle and a great many literary gentlemen used to come to my shop——' He mentioned several—and was thoroughly surprised to learn that I knew them all. At last, I said, that I had once ventured within that charmed circle myself and had printed a book. I saw clearly that I had gained some additional respect from this disclosure.

No one has followed this clue about Keats's relative who was "in business in London". This is probably due in part to the patronising tone adopted by Procter, who contrives, in his own assumption of superiority, to make the bookseller seem a slightly ludicrous character, not to be taken seriously. Yet "Mr. Sheriff Keats", who comes in for Procter's implied disdain, was certainly a real person. The Post Office Directory for 1857 gives him as Sheriff to the City of London in that year, Frederick Keats Esq., residing at No. 182 Piccadilly. Local directories easily identify the bookseller himself. He was Joseph Henry Keats, library and stationer, 107 St. James's Street, Brighton. A search through the London directories confirms his story. He had, in fact, only just moved to Brighton. For over twenty years previous to this, from 1836 to 1857, his bookshop and stationer's business had been in Chelsea, first at 47 Paradise

Row, and later at 142 Sloane Street. He would thus be very handy for Carlyle, whom he specially mentions, and many of the other literary figures of the first half of the nineteenth century.

Since all these circumstantial facts seem to fit, there is no reason to disbelieve Joseph Henry Keats's statement that he was the poet's second cousin. His father was therefore first cousin to Thomas Keats, the poet's father. His name was also Joseph Keats, of 47 Paradise Row, Chelsea, and he was a linen-draper. It is interesting to note that the infrequent appearances of the name "Keats" in the London directories of this time are almost all connected with clothing of one sort or another. The most likely candidate to have been the father of this second Joseph Keats, and therefore Thomas Keats's uncle, is another Joseph Keats, hatter, of 74 Cheapside and also at one time of 12 Pancras Lane. Now Richard Abbey, Keats's guardian, wished him to go into a hat-making business in Cheapside, and the poet actually lodged for a short time at 76 Cheapside, Abbey's tea-broking business being at 4 Pancras Lane. It seems as if this third Joseph Keats was some close relative of the poet—if our conjecture is right, his great-uncle. It is certainly most probable that he was Thomas Keats's uncle. Whether he was established in London before Thomas Keats arrived from the West Country cannot be proved; but the likelihood is that the country lad already had this relative in business in the City.

It may be asked why, if Keats had these business relatives in the City, they are never mentioned by name in his letters. The answer seems to be the contempt which Keats, together with his brothers, had for trade. Keats always applauded his brother George for refusing to continue to work in Richard Abbey's office, and supported him in his quarrel with Abbey's junior partner, Hodgkinson, in a manner which does the poet little credit—he speaks of "Hodgkinson, whose name I cannot bear to write" to their schoolgirl sister, Fanny. He wrote to Benjamin Bailey, when George proposed to emigrate

> This for many reasons has met with my entire consent—and the chief one is this—he is of too independant and liberal a Mind to get on in trade in this Country—in which

> a generous Man with a scanty recourse must be ruined. I would sooner he should till the ground than bow to a Customer—

At almost the same time that these words were written, Keats was satirising in another letter the Corporation of the City of London, with particular reference to one of them, Robert Waithman, himself a linen-draper. Keats certainly had no love for the city gentlemen of his time, and another contemptuous reference of his is interesting, where he remarks "Hodgkinson is more than polite, and the coffee-german endeavour'd to be very close to me the other night". This might be taken to imply that Keats himself had a first cousin (cousin-german) in the coffee business, and it is significant that only a door or two away from Abbey's tea and coffee business, there was a firm of R. & J. Keats, warehousemen.

Later still, when impending illness brought a bitterness to almost everything he wrote, Keats exclaimed to his sister-in-law, George's wife, "Look at our Cheapside Tradesmans sons and daughters —only fit to be taken off by a plague." The "our" of this remark might be taken as a generic term; but with the hat-making establishment of 74 Cheapside in mind, it is more than probable that Keats was thinking of some of his own relatives in trade. All this seems to point to Keats and his father having fairly close relatives in business in the City of London, and to this as a reason why Thomas Keats appears in Town in the early 1790s. It remains to ask where he came from.

II

The clue pointing in this direction is, in its origins, a particularly vague one, as, indeed, are all references to the birthplace of Thomas Keats. A few of Keats's friends, Charles Brown among them, seemed to think he came from Devon, while Fanny Keats, the poet's sister, who was an infant when her father died, said she had heard as a child that he came from Cornwall near Land's End.

The main piece of evidence, however, both circumstantial and yet incomplete, comes from the painter, Joseph Severn, who accompanied Keats to Rome. On September 28th, 1820, the vessel, in which the two men had embarked, put in for the last time on the English coast, and Keats and Severn went for a few hours on shore. This, according to Severn, was at Lulworth Cove, and he continues with a remark that suggests a Dorsetshire origin for the Keats family. On this excursion, "he became" wrote Severn, "like his former self. He was in a part that he already knew, and showed me the splendid caverns and grottoes with a poet's pride, as though they had been his birth-right." Now there is no record of Keats visiting this part of England before in his adult life, so the natural supposition is that he might have stayed with Dorset relatives here while a child, and that this coast was, quite literally, part of his birth-right as the child of a Dorset father. The only drawback to this inference—though, as will be seen, it is a drawback which may have other aspects—is that Severn, on matters of fact, was almost completely unreliable. His own biographer, who quotes this statement, warns the reader of this failing, in the foreword to Severn's Life and Letters. There could not be a less competent witness to what Keats did or said on this last landing on English soil.

It does, however, lead one to look for the birthplace of Thomas Keats somewhere in the eastern half of Dorset. In this direction, there is a circumstantial but intriguing possibility. Both the name of Keats and that of Kates (a local pronunciation) were common in the parish of Milton Abbas, several miles inland and almost due north of Lulworth Cove. There is a circumstance about this parish which may perhaps be thought to give a surprising turn to Severn's story about the Lulworth Cove landing. An extremely interesting feature of the parish of Milton Abbas is that the Abbey Church, after which the place is named, possesses an outlying part of the Dorset coast as a detached portion of the parish of Milton. This is the hamlet of Holworth, described as "the seaside hamlet of Milton", situated, as its name might suggest, on the coast only a few miles to the west of Lulworth. Sixteen miles from the Abbey Church of Milton, it possesses a chapel of its own, and in mediæval times it is said that the monks of Holworth supplied their Abbot at Milton with saltwater fish: hence, at the Reformation, this coastal portion still remained part of the Milton parish—the ecclesiastical parish, that is, for in civil matters Holworth belongs to the neighbouring inland parish of Owermoigne, in whose church there is an inscription to someone "of Holworth, in the parish of Abbotsmilton".

Holworth is an extremely beautiful and lonely coastal spot, with a fine bay for small ships; as such, it is the attractive setting for the smuggling story of one of Thomas Hardy's most engaging Wessex Tales, *The Distracted Preacher*. What is more to the point, it fits Severn's description very much better than the near-by Lulworth. Indeed, the discrepancy between Lulworth and Severn's "splendid caverns and grottoes", even counting the Stair Hole and Durdle Dor, which are not strictly in Lulworth, has already been remarked upon by Sir Sidney Colvin. On the other hand, Holworth Bay has been described by a modern writer in just these terms:

> It would take a boy longer than a summer's holiday to explore all the secret Robin-Hood-retreats of the undercliff, the giddy ledges and castle rocks to be found in that strip of broken ground which extends as far as the blue slopes of shale where the "Holworth volcano" once burned. . . . From the shutter rock, just round the corner of the point, the deep water stretches for only a few yards. Once across this the adventurer is rewarded. Here under the dense weight of White Nose is a very ancient and little-known cave. It requires no great imagination to believe that clear-seen Dorset is the lost island of Ogygia and this cave the hollow cave where the sea nymph Calypso held Ulysses as paramour for seven long years. . . .

Here, rather than Lulworth, was the imaginative playground of a Dorset boy. To mistake Holworth for Lulworth was a minor error compared with many that Severn has perpetrated. Indeed, Holworth, being nearer to Portland Roads, where, according to Keats himself they had hoped to put in that night, is the more likely place altogether. It is, finally, not at all certain that Severn, in his MS. journal of the voyage, ever actually wrote "Lulworth". According to his biographer, he mentions landings at Studland Bay and Dorchester. Dorchester, of course, is not on the coast, but, as we shall go on to see, Holworth is far more closely connected with Dorchester and the Dorset Keatses than Lulworth.

This is half-supported, appropriately enough, by the testimony of another and later poet. It has been seen that Thomas Hardy had a special interest in Holworth; his interest in Keats was also great. He told Sir Sidney Colvin that he knew a family of Dorset Keatses, sprung from a horsedealer of Broadmayne, south-east of Dorchester, members of which bore a striking likeness to the poet. This information, which also appears in Hardy's autobiographical writings, receives the fullest amplification in a letter from Hardy's second wife to Amy Lowell.

> [In Hardy's youth] there was a family named Keats living two or three miles from here [Dorchester], who, Mr. Hardy was told by his father, was a branch of the family of the name living in the direction of Lulworth. . . . They kept horses, being what is called 'hauliers', and did also a little farming. They were in feature singularly like the poet, and were quick-tempered as he is said to have been, one of them being nicknamed 'light-a-fire' on that account. All this is very vague, and may mean nothing, the only arresting point in it considering that they were of the same name, being the facial likeness, which my husband says was very strong. He knew two or three of these Keatses.

Another arresting point, which Mrs. Hardy did not mention, is, of course, the occupation of these Keatses, since Thomas Keats first appears as an ostler. "In the direction of Lulworth" is also significant. Broadmayne, Owermoigne, Holworth, are all close to each other "in the direction of Lulworth" from Dorchester. There is therefore a possibility that Thomas Keats had relatives, or even a major branch of the family, in the Holworth area, with whom Keats, as a boy, might have stayed. This is supported by the fact that only a decade after Keats landed on this part of the coast, there was a Richard Keates—an intermediate spelling of the name—living at Owermoigne.

This explanation cannot, of course, be more than conjectural, since the parish records of Milton Abbas do not contain a Thomas Keats. There is, indeed, a Thomas Kates, and had the poet's father been 36 at his death—the age erroneously given in many biographies—he would have exactly filled the bill. There is, however, another significant circumstance in the history of Milton Abbas. In the early 1780s, the ancient town of Milton with its Grammar School, "the Eton of the West", was razed to the ground by Joseph, Lord Milton, afterwards Earl of Dorchester. His reason for this was merely that its dwellings were too close to his new mansion, though the raids on his property by the Grammar School boys were supposed to be the final straw. At all events, he built the new village of Milton, "a toy town", some way farther off, and proceeded systematically to remove, by fair means or foul, all those villagers who attempted to stay in the old town. Many, in fact, did not move to the new village, but left the district for other parts of Dorset, or even farther afield. Among these are known to have been the families of both Keats and Kates, whose names henceforward cease to appear in the new Milton.

In the next generation, there do appear, however, in north-east Dorset and over the Wiltshire border two brothers, James and Thomas Keats, born in 1815 and 1816 respectively, the sons of James Keats, a coachman. One of these brothers, James, afterwards Clerk to the Justices at Usk-on-Wye, was certainly educated at Shaftesbury, which school, as well as that of Blandford, took on the functions of the murdered establishment at Milton Abbas. This Thomas Keats's descendants kept the family name of Thomas through three generations. It is to the present Thomas Augustus Keats that I owe this information, and photographs of his elder son show a remarkable likeness to the features of the poet.

There are thus two independent appearances of families of Keatses, one in south-east, the other in north-east Dorset, both strongly resembling the poet and both connected with horses or coaching, the profession of the poet's father. It is reasonable to connect these with the dispersal of Keatses and Kateses from Milton Abbas, the centre of this area, and to conjecture this place or nearabouts as the original home of the poet's family.

There is thus a reason, if this conjecture be accepted, why Thomas Keats should appear in London; why his family history should be obscure; why Keats should say of the name

> Enchanted has it been the Lord knows where.

A young countryman forcibly deprived of his family background, seeking perhaps some branch of relatives who were already in London, Thomas Keats may appear less of a

Holworth in 1827

Frontispiece to Chatterton's Rowley Poems

mystery than he has been reckoned. The intense clannishness of his family, the feeling, which Keats and his brothers undoubtedly possessed, that they were set apart from other people, may also be explained. There was a fierce independence about the Milton people, which may mitigate, though it can hardly condone, the harshness of Lord Milton's action. Thomas Hardy characterised Milton Abbas as being a place where one might gain strength, "particularly strength of mind". If this account of Keats's ancestry is accepted, in spite of some links which still remain circumstantial, it may do much to explain that obstinacy and determination of purpose which is bound up in every way with the character of the poet himself.

7

KEATS AND CHATTERTON

To Hyder E. Rollins

THE connection between Keats and Chatterton is such an obvious one, and so fully vouched for, both by Keats himself and by his friends, that at first sight there would appear to be no problem in it. However, when one studies carefully the poems of Keats alongside the poems of Chatterton, one or two curious and interesting facts begin to emerge. Very briefly, they are these:

(1) Although Keats seems to have first read Chatterton in the autumn of 1815, not a single line of his own first volume, published in the spring of 1817, shows the slightest poetic influence of Chatterton.

(2) Although continuing to read and indeed recite Chatterton in the later part of 1817, nothing in *Endymion*, composed in that year, shows any trace of Chatterton's style.

(3) A more conscious interest in the style of Chatterton, whose cause will be discussed below, seems to have taken place in the spring of 1818. To this time belong at least one lyric which echoes exactly a lyric by Chatterton, and the dedication of *Endymion*, four months after its completion, to a poet who seems to have had singularly little to do with it.

(4) In January and February, 1819, during an intensive spell of writing, the style of Chatterton, with many verbal echoes, occurs in every poem, major or minor, which Keats writes, and, as suddenly, disappears again from his work.

(5) In the middle of September, 1819, Keats not only returns to the style of Chatterton, with verbal echoes, but extols that style in his letters.

Before trying to explain and expand this sequence of events, one note of warning must be sounded. The only exact proof of the influence of Chatterton on Keats is still missing. This is his own annotated copy. No trace of it was found in the "Chest of Books" belonging to him at his death. It seems inconceivable that he should not have had a personal copy, and it is equally conceivable that it may one day turn up. In the meantime we should, I think, accept Professor Rollins's supposition that Keats's copy of Chatterton was the 1803 three-volume edition. Charles Cowden Clarke possessed a copy of this, which is now in the Keats Museum, Hampstead. It contains a characteristic MS. annotation, in the shape of a furious attack on Chatterton's editors by Benjamin Robert Haydon, who had presumably borrowed the book at one time. Richard Woodhouse, too, seems to have been as familiar with Chatterton's life and work as was Keats himself. He, like Keats, linked Chatterton with Shakespeare. The three-volume edition, then, seems to have been common to several people in the Keats circle; it also seems likely that the volume most quoted and discussed among them was Volume II, "containing the poems attributed to Rowley".

The first evidence of Keats's reading in these volumes is found in November 1815, the date given in the 1817 *Poems* to his *Epistle to George Felton Mathew*, whom he addresses in lines 53–58:

> Yet this is vain—O Mathew lend thy aid
> To find a place where I may greet the maid—
> Where we may soft humanity put on,
> And sit, and rhyme and think on Chatterton;
> And that warm-hearted Shakespeare sent to meet him
> Four laurell'd spirits, heaven-ward to intreat him.

This is confirmed by the sonnet, rejected for the 1817 volume, to Chatterton himself. Woodhouse dates this as composed in 1815. It is very much in the style of the *Epistle*, and its eighth line, "A half-blown flow'ret which cold blasts amate", echoes both the *Epistle*, in which Mathew himself is also called a flowret, and the archaism of the Rowley poems. Its first lines are also modelled on the poems to Chatterton printed in the editor's introduction to Volume I of the three-volume edition. "O Chatterton! How very sad thy fate!" echoes these poems, which abound in exclamations of "Oh Chatterton!", "Ah Chatterton!" and even "Poor Chatterton!" There is, however, no touch of Chatterton's style in the *Poems* published in 1817, and only one other possible passing reference to him, in *Sleep and Poetry*, lines 218–219, as belonging

> To some lone spirits who could proudly sing
> Their youth away, and die.

1817, the *Endymion* year, is the year referred to in the most concrete outside evidence we have of Keats's love of Chatterton, the comment of Benjamin Bailey:

> Every one now (1849) knows what was then (1817) known to his friends, that Keats was an ardent admirer of Chatterton. The melody of the verses of "the marvellous Boy who perished in his pride," enchanted the author of Endymion. Methinks I now hear him recite, or *chant*, in his peculiar manner, the following stanza of the "Roundelay sung by the minstrels of Ella:"
>
> "*Come with acorn cup & thorn,*
> Drain my hertys blood away;
> Life & all its goods I scorn;
> Dance by night or feast by day."
>
> The first line to his ear possessed the great charm.

"The great charm", however, of Chatterton's style does not appear anywhere in *Endymion*, which is largely dominated by the greater charm of Shakespeare.

It appears to have been Hazlitt who, by his depreciation, aroused in Keats a more conscious appreciation of Chatterton. On February 21st, 1818, Keats wrote, "I hear Hazlitt's lectures regularly . . . I was very disappointed at his treatment of Chatterton." Dorothy Hewlett conjectures that Keats may have been in part referred to in the apology with which Hazlitt prefaced his next lecture, where the lecturer went on to quote and praise the very stanza which was so much a favourite with Keats. Certainly, within a month, Keats himself paid Chatterton several indirect tributes. On Saturday, March 14th, 1818, he wrote the lines which begin with the stanza

> Where be ye going, you Devon Maid?
> And what have ye there in the Basket?
> Ye tight little fairy just fresh from the dairy,
> Will ye give me some cream if I ask it?

This and the remaining stanzas are based on another "Mynstrelles songe" from Chatterton's *Ælla*, in which the second stanza runs

> Mie husbande, Lorde Thomas, a forrester boulde,
> As ever clove pynne, or the baskette,
> Does no cherysauncys from Elynour houlde,
> I have ytte as soone as I aske ytte.

Another lively lyric at this time (March 25th), "Over the hill and over the dale", contains the line "Say's I hold your tongue you young Gipsey". This suggests that Keats was also reading Chatterton's *The Revenge—a Burletta*, where Bacchus, hoping to ravish Maia, as he thinks, lays his preparations in similar terms, and uses the line, "For should the little gipsy make resistance."

A more conscious tribute was, of course, Keats's dedication of *Endymion* to Chatterton. In its original form this read:

> Inscribed
> with every feeling of pride and regret
> and with "a bowed mind",
> To the memory of
> The most english of Poets except Shakespeare,
> Thomas Chatterton—

This was written, half-way between the two Devon lyrics and also at Teignmouth, on Thursday, March 19th, 1818. At this time Keats was in the middle of composing *Isabella*. This poem is very far from the style of Chatterton; yet there is an interesting connection, which seems to have been unnoticed till now. Keats's favourite "Mynstrelles songe" from *Ælla* begins "O! synge untoe mie Roundelaie", and each stanza ends with the chorus

> Mie love ys dedde,
> Gon to hys deathe-bedde,
> Al under the wyllowe tree.

In *Isabella* the tragedy of the heroine finding the buried corpse of her lover begins in stanza XXXII, which contains the significant expression "a roundelay Of death". Keats proceeds to elaborate the finding of the corpse for sixteen more stanzas, and then breaks off

> Ah! wherefore all this wormy circumstance?
> Why linger at the yawning tomb so long?
> O for the gentleness of old Romance,
> The simple plaining of a minstrel's song!

It is extremely likely that "a minstrel's song", which was at first written "*the* minstrel's song", was one which was actually present in Keats's mind, the "mynstrelles songe" from *Ælla*. The song does indeed, without the "wormy circumstance" of the poem, cover the same ground in a gentle and simple lyric series of short stanzas. The stanza from Chatterton specially loved and quoted by Keats has much parallel, in feeling and meaning, with the famous stanza LIII of *Isabella*, beginning "And she forgot the stars, the moon, and sun", while, at the conclusion to the lyric, as with the heroine of *Isabella*, "Thos the damselle spake and dyed".

There is, however, no hint of Chatterton in the sonnets and lyrics written by Keats during his Scottish tour of summer, 1818, nor in the first two books of *Hyperion* written in the autumn of that year. Cary's translation of the *Inferno*, Shakespeare and Milton dominate these months, which end with four events all of great influence on Keats's poetry—his resumed acquaintanceship with Mrs. Isabella Jones, his meeting with Fanny Brawne, the death of his brother Tom, and his removal to Wentworth Place. Early in the New Year he took up *Hyperion* again. The very great alteration in style of the unfinished Book III of this poem has been remarked upon, but its most likely source does not seem to have been noticed. To show what this may be, it is necessary to quote some twenty-eight lines of Keats, and two short passages from Chatterton's Rowley poems; Keats's lines are from the address to the Muse, and the description of Apollo's surroundings.

> Flush every thing that hath a vermeil hue,
> Let the rose glow intense and warm the air,
> And let the clouds of even and of morn
> Float in voluptuous fleeces o'er the hills;

Let the red wine within the goblet boil,
Cold as a bubbling well; let faint-lipp'd shells,
On sands, or in great deeps, vermilion turn
Through all their labyrinths; and let the maid
Blush keenly, as with some warm kiss surpris'd.
Chief isle of the embowered Cyclades,
Rejoice, O Delos, with thine olives green,
And poplars, and lawn-shading palms, and beech,
In which the Zephyr breathes the loudest song,
And hazels thick, dark-stemm'd beneath the shade:
Apollo is once more the golden theme!
Where was he, when the Giant of the Sun
Stood bright, amid the sorrow of his peers?
Together had he left his mother fair
And his twin-sister sleeping in their bower,
And in the morning twilight wandered forth
Beside the osiers of a rivulet,
Full ankle-deep in lilies of the vale.
The nightingale had ceas'd, and a few stars
Were lingering in the heavens, while the thrush
Began calm-throated. Throughout all the isle
There was no covert, no retired cave
Unhaunted by the murmurous noise of waves,
Though scarcely heard in many a green recess.

These lines may be read side by side with two passages from Chatterton, the first his description of the beautiful Kenewalcha in the *Battle of Hastings*:

White as the chaulkie clyffes of Brittaines isle,
Red as the highest colour'd Gallic wine,
Gaie as all nature at the mornynge smile,
Those hues with pleasaunce on her lippes combine,
Her lippes more redde than summer evenynge skyne,
Or Phoebus rysinge in a frostie morne,
Her breste more white than snow in feeldes that lyene,
Or lillie lambes that never have been shorne,
Swellynge like bubbles in a boillynge welle,
Or new-braste brooklettes gently whyspringe in the delle.

The second passage is the beginning of *The Storie of William Canynge*:

Anent a brooklette as I laie reclynd,
Listeynge to heare the water glyde alonge,
Myndeynge how thorowe the grene mees yt twynd,
Awhilst the cavys respons'd yts mottring songe,
At dystaunt rysyng Avonne to be sped,
Amenged wyth rysyng hylles dyd shewe yts head;

Engarlanded wyth crownes of osyer weedes.

Keats's lines borrow their cadence, their feeling, and their images from these two passages, the most notable likeness being in his lines

Let the red wine within the goblet boil
Cold as a bubbling well;

Another borrowing from the same source may perhaps be seen in the verses of *Hush, hush* to "Isabel"

Who dances on bubbles where brooklets meet.

It is perhaps dangerous to attribute too much influence by Chatterton on *The Eve of St. Agnes*, begun at the same time, about January 21st, 1819. The frequent "Rowley" archaisms in this poem, such as "argent", "mickle", "all amort" and so on, might equally have been suggested by the Spenserian stanza in which the poem is written; yet the feeling is not unlike much of Chatterton, and Porphyro's breathless adoration of Madeline has some counterpart in later stanzas of the same *Storie of William Canynge*, whose opening has been quoted above.

Astounded mickle there I sylente laie,
Still scauncing wondrous at the walkynge syghte;
Mie senses forgarde ne coulde reyn awaie;
But was ne forstraughte when shee dyd alyghte
Anie to me, dreste up yn naked viewe,

. . . .

I lok'd wyth eyne as pure as angelles doe.

Then too, the "black purgatorial rails" of *St. Agnes* may well have been suggested by those in the frontispiece of Volume II, portraying "The Base of the Tower of Redcliff Church, with a view of the Muniment Room over the North Porch".

The most obvious borrowing from Chatterton, perhaps this time deliberate, is in the fragment of *The Eve of St. Mark*, composed February 13th to 17th, 1819. Keats has taken the name of his heroine, Bertha, from the heroine of Chatterton's *Ælla*. The opening of the poem and its metre come from Chatterton's *The Unknown Knight or The Tournament*:

> The Matten belle han sounded long,
> The Cocks han sang their morning songe,

while Bertha's book,

> A curious volume, patched and torn,

echoes

> And on each sheelde devices shone,
> Of wounded hearts and battles won,
> All curious and nice echon;

of the same poem. Moreover Keats includes in his poem a deliberate "imitation of the Authors in Chaucer's time", more skilful in its way than most of Chatterton's "Rowley" imitations.

The influences on Keats's style throughout the following summer are mostly to be found in Robert Burton and Dryden; Keats began "much study" of the latter's "versification" about the middle of April, and continued to read deeply in both these authors till the autumn. A dramatic break in his regular programme of "study" and writing occurred on the evening of Friday, September 10th, when he was alone at Winchester. Hearing that his brother George was in serious financial straits in America, he took the night coach to London to raise funds. He was not too successful. "Every body was out", and the most profitable result of his visit was half a day spent with Woodhouse on Sunday, September 12th. He returned to Winchester on Wednesday, the 15th, and on Sunday, the 19th, he composed the *Ode to Autumn*. Here, as is well known, he not only echoed in great detail yet another "Mynstrelles songe" from *Ælla*, the one beginning "Whanne Autumpne blake and sonnebrente doe appere", but paid conscious tribute to the style of Chatterton in his letters written on Tuesday, the 21st. "He is the purest writer in the English Language" (*Letters*, 151), "The purest english I think—or what ought to be the purest—is Chatterton's" (*Letters*, 156). Yet Chatterton then disappears from his writing, this time for ever. The ejaculation "Ah hertè mine", scribbled at the bottom of his letter to Fanny Brawne on October 11th, is taken from Troilus's complaint to Cressida in Book V of Chaucer's *Troilus and Criseyde*, whose other stanzas are all echoed in the four passionate poems he poured out to Fanny at this time. Chaucer, not "Rowley", now absorbs him, as he sees himself in the character of Chaucer's hero, and Fanny as Cressida. Although the character "Bertha" reappears in his last unhappy comic poem, *The Cap and Bells*, she is only a borrowing from the unfinished *Eve of St. Mark*, and has nothing to do with Chatterton.

Any interpretation of the appearances in Keats's style of the other young and tragic poet must, of course, land us in conjecture. I have suggested that Hazlitt's slighting remarks may, by reaction, have caused Keats's imitation and championship of Chatterton in the spring of 1818. What is the interpretation of the events of 1819? Clearly, Chatterton is very close to Keats in the first seven weeks of that year, and then suddenly appears again in his consciousness after the visit to London in the middle of September. These coincidences may be fortuitous, or they may have factors in common. One quite tenable theory is that Keats was reading Chatterton with Isabella Jones. He was seeing much of her early in 1819; he had hoped, he said, to instruct her "in matters of knowledge and taste". *The Eve of St. Agnes* was written on her suggestion, she was the "Isabel" of *Hush, hush*, and her room seems to be portrayed in *The Eve of St. Mark*. She may have been one of the many people he found to be not at home when he paid his September visit to London, for she had gone that summer to take the cure at Tunbridge Wells. Had he left his copy of Chatterton in her rooms at 34 Gloucester Street, and did he rescue it on that occasion? Those who believe that the poems mentioned were inspired by Fanny Brawne may claim that Fanny had some connection with Keats's reading of Chatterton. A final and perhaps less romantic conjecture may connect the whole matter with Woodhouse. Keats was seeing a good deal of the literary lawyer early in 1819, and he spent much of September 12th in his company. Chatterton must have been a frequent matter of discussion and quotation between the two men, and it is perhaps to Woodhouse that we owe the final flowering of Keats's devotion to "the most english of Poets" in his own *Ode to Autumn*.

8

"MOST ENORMOUS CAF"

To M. R. Ridley

MOST poets, and indeed most readers, who have once fallen under the spell of Milton, will have found themselves specially affected by the sonorous ring of his great lists of names: whether of places,

> Jousted in *Aspramont* or *Montalban*,
> *Damasco*, or *Marocco*, or *Trebisond*,
> Or whom *Biserta* sent from *Afric* shore

or of persons,

> Blind *Thamyris* and blind *Mæonides*,
> And *Tiresias* and *Phineus* Prophets old.

Keats, writing of his own *Hyperion*, acknowledged that the poem was full of Miltonisms; among such he must surely have been thinking of the recital of the names of "the bruised Titans", which begins Book II. Apart from Hyperion himself, who has been displayed in his fiery palace in the latter part of Book I, the first hundred lines of this second book contain over twenty names of mythological persons. In one place, the lines are solid with them.

> Cœus, and Gyges, and Briareus,
> Typhon, and Dolor, and Porphyrion,

For this impressive catalogue, however, Keats would not need to go particularly far in his own reading of Lempriere's Classical Dictionary and Sandys's translation of Ovid's Metamorphoses, while he had just borrowed from Richard Woodhouse the poems of Ronsard, in which he would have found a similar conjunction of giant syllables.

Ici Phébus d'un trait qu'il jette
Fit Encelade trébucher,
Là Porphyre lui fit broncher . . .

In this classical array, the show-piece of Keats's most classical poem, which even his harshest critic, Lord Byron, compared with Æschylus, there is one unaccountable non-classical stranger, unashamedly oriental. This is Caf, whom Keats designates as the male parent of Asia in the line

Asia, born of most enormous Caf,

Who or what is Caf, a name unknown in Lempriere or in any of Keats's classical sources, unknown, it may be said, anywhere in this particular spelling except in this particular line 53 of *Hyperion*, Book II? Did Keats merely invent it, or has it some origin which we may trace and, in tracing, come surprisingly near to a hardly-noticed source for the scene and setting of the whole of this part of the poem?*

First, why did Keats import this name at all? He had many classical names ready among those of the Greek gods, giants and Titans; they are, indeed, almost embarrassingly prolific of parents and relations. Helped by Apollodorus, or some such source, one usually has the pick of about three possible fathers or mothers for any one child. The general opinion, which Keats could have found in Lempriere, is that Asia was one of the Oceanides, a child of the sea-god Oceanus by his consort Tethys, though in *Hyperion* he makes her mother to be Tellus, the earth-mother. Yet, though Oceanus and Tethys appear later in the poem with their daughter Clymene, there is no suggestion of any relationship with Asia; it was evidently not this origin for her upon which Keats's mind was working. The clue almost certainly lies in another entry in Lempriere. This is under Cotys, a name given several attributions, the first of which, and therefore the most likely to catch Keats's eye, being "father of Asia", and the authority cited being Herodotus. In point of fact, Lempriere had mistaken what Herodotus said. In one of his characteristic digressions (Book IV, chapter 45) he remarks that the Greeks always reckon that the continent of Asia was named after the Oceanid Asia. The Lydians, however, says Herodotus, as a matter of local pride and patriotism,

*Except for M. R. Ridley, *Keats' Craftsmanship*, pp. 62*n*. & 270–271.

trace the name from Asies, the son of Cotys, who was a Lydian king.

Keats did not read Herodotus, and would not have known this; there is a good reason to believe that he took Lempriere's word, and that Cotys was the name that first entered his mind. This reason lies in the fact that once he had thought of the name Cotys, he would have had to discard it for purely poetic purposes. The four lines immediately before, in this section of *Hyperion*, had named, and been concerned with the Titan Cottus. His name probably suggested Cotys to Keats, a suggestion to be almost at once rejected when his ear recognised the clash of syllables. This does not appear in the manuscript, but there is an almost exact parallel in stanza vii of the *Ode to a Nightingale*, where "the sad heart of Ruth" suggested, three lines later, the adjective in "ruthless seas", which was quickly corrected to the famous "perilous".

The process, we can guess, went something like this. The name Asia itself suggested something oriental. Keats had a taste, which he shared with the rest of his age, for oriental tales. He mentions one "of a very beautiful color", which he read the following summer. For the name—though not the spelling —he would not have needed to have gone any further in oriental literature than the Koran; one of the Suras, or chapters of the Koran, is actually named Kaf. There is no certainty, however, that this section is named after a person or a place. Kaf, in this context, may not be a name at all, but a collection of initials, or a monogram appended to the manuscript of this particular Sura by an owner or a copyist. A collection of initials seems to be a dubious parent for Asia, and, in any case, there is no evidence that Keats ever read the Koran. On the other hand, there is one special oriental tale, popular in his time, which he certainly read, and in which the name Kaf plays a dominant and memorable part.

This is *The History of the Caliph Vathek* by that notable figure William Beckford. This remarkable book, written originally in French, at the age of 22, and at a single sitting lasting three days and four nights, is one of the most successful curiosities of English literature. It contrives to be, at the same time, a tale of oriental extravagance and fancy in the fashionable manner, and a delightful high-spirited parody of all such stories. In this tale of the pleasure-loving Caliph, who, with his bride and his wicked mother, ends up in the eternal torments of the halls of Eblis, Beckford very cleverly keeps pushing the oriental details of feast, harem, and massacre a little over the brink of absurdity, without ever making them merely a comic skit. There is fine writing in many of the descriptions, especially, as we shall see, in the final account of the infernal halls of Eblis, and it is just this kind of romantic writing that appealed to Keats, wherever he found it.

Keats was undoubtedly an appreciative reader of *Vathek*. The most positive proof is in his letters. Writing to J. H. Reynolds about the tedious curator of the cottage where Burns was born, Keats exclaims, "I sho[d] like to employ Caliph Vatheck to kick him——". This is an allusion to the habits of Beckford's hero, who, whenever thwarted, used to kick the objects of his displeasures, even, in one instance, after they were dead.

> In the paroxysm of his passion he fell furiously
> on the poor carcases, and kicked them till
> evening without intermission.

Apart from this direct reference, there are indirect allusions among Keats's poems. Sir Sidney Colvin, indeed, claimed that the mysterious caverns visited by Endymion in Book II of that poem were inspired by *Vathek*, though on close examination there seems to be little resemblance, verbal or otherwise. More concrete is the line in Keats's letter-poem to J. H. Reynolds (25 March 1818) describing part of a castle as

> Built by a banish'd Santon of Chaldee:

The Santons were a race of holy men who appear in *Vathek*; they too suffer kicking and other indignities by order of the Caliph. It may also be thought that some of the oriental colour, which Keats himself parodied in *The Cap and Bells*, was derived, whether consciously or not, from *Vathek*. The Emperor in this humorous poem is a capricious monarch like Vathek, with the same passions and hints of the bowstring to his menials. He is addressed, like Vathek, as "Commander of the

Faithful". Moreover the description of the birth of the Emperor's loved one is distinctly like *Vathek*.

> Her mother's screams with the striped tiger's blent,
> While the torch-bearing slaves a halloo sent
> Into the jungles; and her palanquin,
> Rested amid the desert's dreariment,
> Shook with her agony,

This recalls at once the trials of Vathek's great expedition in the "dreary prospects" of the wild country it traverses by night. Its "palanquins"—the same word—are surrounded by howling tigers, and only the lighting of "ten thousand torches" saves the shrieking wives of Vathek, who travel in them.

It is clear that Keats was familiar with *Vathek*, and it is in this story that the name Kaf plays a dominant part. It is the mountain of Kaf—hence "most enormous" Kaf—whose subterranean recesses are approached from the halls of Eblis, ruler of the underworld, and which forms an oriental hell. Here the impious Caliph finds Soliman Ben Daoud and the other "preadamite" kings, whose glories he aspires to share, only to discover that he must also share with them their eternal torments. This description of the interior of Kaf is the most impressive portion of the book, primitively grand and just suited to Keats's Titanic purpose. This is not to suggest that he re-read *Vathek* while writing *Hyperion*; the spelling of Caf with a C might suggest that he did not, though this is probably derived from another memory of *Vathek*. The Caliph's wicked mother has a gigantic female slave named Cafour, and this lady and the mountain probably combined in the name that Keats wrote. That a mountain should have been the father of Asia was also probably suggested to his mind by the fact that Asia herself was the mother of Atlas.

To trace the origins of a single word in a long epic like *Hyperion* may seem at worst a cul-de-sac of scholarship, and at best a mere sidelight on Keats's way of composition; but in this instance it may be shown to have a far wider significance. It can be a clue which leads to the whole background of this part of the poem in Keats's mind. His own statement that he gave up the poem because it was written in too Miltonic a style has for long misled critics, who have tried to find parallels between it and *Paradise Lost*. The fact is that neither the setting of the fiery halls of Hyperion in the second part of Book I, nor of the dark abode of the Titans in the early part of Book II is at all like Milton, although, as Keats said, there are "too many Miltonic inversions" in the style. Modern commentators have begun to realise this, and to explore other regions of Keats's reading, which contributed to these two strongly-painted sets of epic scenery. An attempt has been made to point to likenesses between Hyperion's palace and the golden sky-scape described by Wordsworth in Book II of *The Excursion*, a poem which Keats admired, though, on a careful reading, the parallels prove to be very slight. More certainly Keats drew some of the damp, cold, dark atmosphere of the Titans' den from a re-reading of his own letters describing the Scottish mountains, where he had gone on his walking-tour earlier in the year 1818, and which he himself said would serve as inspiration in the epic poem, for which he was even then fitting himself. I have myself suggested elsewhere that some of the details of the Titans' den may have been derived from Malebolge in Dante's *Inferno*, and some of the debates of the Titans from the councils of the Greeks and Trojans in *Troilus and Cressida*, both of which, it can be proved, he was reading at the time he composed this part of *Hyperion*.

No one has, however, suggested before that both the palace of Hyperion and the den of the imprisoned Titans have a common source, which is as far removed as possible from Milton; that, in fact, not only the imagery of both, but the sequence in which the reader is led from one to the other, owe their origin to the closing pages of Beckford's *Vathek*. With this new explanation of the word Caf to point the way, we may see how close the sequence and the imagery is.

First, we may examine what occurs in the final 3,000 words of *Vathek*, which, most critics agree, are a tour-de-force of atmospheric writing. The Caliph Vathek and his bride Nouronihar having renounced the teaching of Mahomet, arrive to receive their reward from Eblis, the Lord of the Underworld. They first enter the halls of Eblis, which, though subterranean, are described as flaming and brilliant.

The Caliph and Nouronihar beheld each other with

amazement, at finding themselves in a place which, though roofed with a vaulted ceiling, was so spacious and lofty that at first they took it for an immeasurable plain. But their eyes at length growing familiar to the grandeur of the objects at hand, they extended their view to those at a distance, and discovered rows of columns and arcades, which gradually diminished till they terminated in a point, radiant as the sun when he darts his last beams athwart the ocean; the pavement, strewed over with gold dust and saffron, exhaled so subtle an odour as almost overpowered them; they, however, went on, and observed an infinity of censers, in which ambergris and the wood of aloes were continually burning; between the several columns were placed tables, each spread with a profusion of viands, and wines of every species sparkling in vases of crystal. A throng of Genii and other fantastic spirits of each sex danced in troops, at the sound of music which issued from beneath . . . They continued their way through the multitude; but, notwithstanding their confidence at first, they were not sufficiently composed to examine with attention the various perspectives of halls and of galleries that opened on the right hand and left, which were all illuminated by torches and braziers, whose flames rose in pyramids to the centre of the vault. At length they came to a place where long curtains, brocaded with crimson and gold, fell from all parts in striking confusion . . .

In *Hyperion*, Book I, Keats described Hyperion's palace.

His palace bright
Bastion'd with pyramids of glowing gold,
And touch'd with shades of bronzed obelisks,
Glar'd a blood-red through all its thousand courts,
Arches, and domes, and fiery galleries;
And all its curtains of Aurorian clouds
Flush'd angerly:

and again

On he flared
From stately nave to nave, from vault to vault,
Through bowers of fragrant and enwreathed light,
And diamond-paved lustrous long arcades,

The fiery vaults, galleries, arcades (an unusual word) and halls, the pyramids of flame and the glowing curtains, the troops of attendants, the incense and the pavements strewn with precious objects form a picture which is echoed by the poem. Like Hyperion, Vathek and Nouronihar are described a little later as wandering "on from hall to hall", the exact words which Keats uses in the poem to express Hyperion's "stride colossal".

Yet it is the sequence of their adventures that suggests the poem even more strongly than the verbal resemblances. Having first explored these fiery galleries, they then meet Eblis himself. He is described as young, weary, "tarnished by malignant vapours", just as Hyperion battles with "heavy vapours"; this all recalls the description, though not the exact words of Keats, just as Eblis, sitting "upon a globe of fire" at once brings to mind how

> Blazing Hyperion on his orbed fire
> Still sat . . .

It is difficult not to believe that the weary sun-god and his bright but hateful courts were taken from Eblis and his fiery halls filled with despair, especially as the adventures of Vathek and Nouronihar continue. Eblis announces to them that his halls lead to the subterranean caverns of the mountain of Kaf. They enter these, and are at once in a completely different atmosphere; the caverns are dark and gloomy, and

> the sullen roar of a vast cataract was . . .
> the only sound that intruded on the silence
> of these doleful mansions.

So in *Hyperion*, Book II,

> It was a den where no insulting light
> Could glimmer on their tears; where their own groans
> They felt, but heard not, for the solid roar
> Of thunderous waterfalls and torrents hoarse,

Here they meet "the pre-adamite kings", stretched on their sides for eternity, and learn from the greatest of them, Soliman Ben Daoud, that they too are damned. He

> laboured with profound sighs, and, like his companions, kept his right hand on his heart.

Keats's Titans

> Were pent in regions of laborious breath;
> Dungeon'd in opaque element, to keep
> Their clenched teeth still clench'd, and all their limbs
> Lock'd up like veins of metal, crampt and screw'd;
> Without a motion, save of their big hearts . . .

The reason is explained by Soliman. Their punishment is that their hearts are turned to burning fire, like the hearts of Keats's Titans,

> Heaving in pain, and horribly convuls'd
> With sanguine feverous boiling gurge of pulse.

This torture turns all who suffer it to hate their former companions.

> Some stalked slowly on, absorbed in profound reverie; some, shrieking with agony, ran furiously about, like tigers wounded with poisoned arrows; whilst others, grinding their teeth in rage, foamed along, more frantic than the wildest maniac. They all avoided each other, and, though surrounded by a multitude that no one could number, each wandered at random, unheedful of the rest, as if alone on a desert which no foot had trodden.

Keats says of his Titans

> Each one kept shroud, nor to his neighbour gave
> Or word, or look, or action of despair.

They are described as violent, full of rage and passion; the huge Enceladus in particular is described by Keats as "tiger-passion'd", a strange compound, unconsciously suggested by the oriental imagery of this part of *Vathek*.

It may, of course, be argued that when any writer describes a set of infernal regions, he is likely to draw upon a common stock of conventional imagery; there are bound to be fiery furnaces, gloom, and a certain amount of weeping, wailing, and gnashing of teeth. What connects Keats's picture of the Titans so closely with Beckford's vision is the particular sequence in which both lead the reader. In both, and in the same order, there are two regions, one of brilliant, metallic light, music, attendant spirits, and long vistas of architecture, the other dark, damp, cramped, rocky and soundless, except for the continual pouring of unseen waters. The connecting figure, in each case, is a sad, tarnished, and godlike giant, whose keynote is not energy or defiance (as with Milton's Satan) but much more of an uneasy melancholy.

This, interesting in itself, becomes much more so when we look at its general application to poetic writing. Beckford's book was the kind of jeu d'esprit which Keats particularly appreciated, and which certain of his friends, notably Charles Brown, were always trying to write, a work combining the popular elements of oriental luxuriance, horror, and extravagant humour. On the other hand it is not major and epic reading, and cannot compare with Keats's deliberate "study", to use his own word, of *Paradise Lost* or of Dante's *Inferno*. Yet, it would seem, its arrangement and dramatic images, when he began to enter deeply into his own epic, held a sway over parts of his composition which has never been noticed before; although Dante, Milton, and Shakespeare dominate the opening of Keats's poem, these long middle sections owe much to the comparatively minor gifts of Beckford. It is, in fact, one more example of the fascinating way in which a major writer can feed on a minor work, and, by the poetic metabolism of his own constitution, completely transform it for his own wider purposes. It is only an occasional unassimilated and undigested morsel—in this instance, the solitary mention of "most enormous Caf"—which hints at the type of nourishment a poet's casual reading can give to his creative mind.

9

COUSIN MARY AND KEATS'S HYACINTH

To H. C. Brooke-Taylor

THE title of a new poem by Keats, though the poem itself be lost, is well worth recording. The ways of MSS. are strange, and it may be that this recital of the known facts about it may one day bring to light the unknown work—*The Hyacinth*. That this was its title, or at least its subject, appears from an authority not previously available—the letters to John Taylor, Keats's publisher, from his lively and intelligent cousin, Mary Drury.

Mary Drury was the youngest girl among the seven children of James W. Drury, bookseller, of Lincoln, the brother of John Taylor's mother. Taylor, leaving his partner Hessey in charge at Fleet Street, was in the habit of paying regular summer visits to his own family in Nottinghamshire and frequently broke his journey to see his "Lincoln relatives". James Drury's illness and death in 1815 occasioned the first letter from Cousin Mary to "Dear Cousin John". At that time in her early twenties, she was a successful governess, happily teaching French, Music and Drawing to the daughters of a Mrs. Ambler in Yorkshire; now the worst fate of the only unmarried daughter was to be hers. She was to return to Lincoln to companion her widowed mother, while her brother, John, took over the library and book-selling business. The new restriction of this life made her turn eagerly to correspond with her London cousin, in touch with the latest publications. By the beginning of 1817, they were exchanging letters regularly once a month and discussing, in particular, "modern" poetry—"Wordsworth is neither in our Library, nor in the Shop, therefore I must again trespass on your time and good nature to transcribe for me the parts you mention". In her turn, she gives charming and Jane Austen-like descriptions of local doings, notably a "Cake Ball" or Twelfth Night dance.

In April 1817 a new note creeps in, though its cause is not at first defined. John Taylor is "almost my only correspondent now" and his "sensible, indulgent and refined letter" each month is an antidote to depression. Modern poetry is still a main topic between the cousins: she compares Wordsworth's *Daisy* with Burns's: "Wordsworth is not a favourite of mine. I think his style affected to a degree, childish and ridiculous, yet think in this case he has succeeded *in his way*, as well as Burns" —nor is modern prose neglected: Godwin's *Caleb Williams* is "a grandly terrible book". Yet some personal problem is undoubtedly weighing on her; her cousin's visit that summer emboldens her to trust him with it in a manner once more reminiscent of Jane Austen, and on a matter which turns out to have considerable indirect connection with Keats and the lost poem.

One of Mary Drury's elder sisters, Elizabeth, had been married for some years to a Mr. John Tallant. The families were connected by more than marriage. Michael Drury, one of Mary's brothers, had a bookselling business in Philadelphia, in which he was partnered by a younger Tallant brother, James. Even before her sister's wedding, Mary Drury and James Tallant had felt, as Mary puts it, "a mutual sympathy", and now before departing to America, he had come forward as her suitor. The results were unhappy for Mary. Mrs. Drury, at once opposed to her only unmarried daughter leaving home, put her foot down; besides, the young man had not enough money. Mary was forbidden even to see her brother Michael; John and Elizabeth Tallant were not to interfere; if James Tallant returned to England and tried to visit the house John Drury was to throw him out. All this news Mary entrusted to John Taylor, together with a pencilled note to be forwarded by him to her lover—"To Jas. Tallant—Try my Mother—try more than once—let M[ichae]l direct your letters, else they will not be opened—state that you have heard injurious, cruel reports of me—that you disbelieve them all—that you humbly and *afresh* offer yourself as my Protector——"

This scribbled note was instantly followed by another, begging John Taylor not to send the "letter for America".

Mary had given in to her mother. "I am very *good now*", she wrote to her cousin, although regretfully quoting Burns

> Oh! why should fate such pleasure have
> Life's dearest bonds untwining,
> Oh! why so sweet a flower as Love
> Depend on fortune's shining?

"Put this on your fire and *taisez vous*," she concludes.

Her confidant obeyed the second injunction, but added to it a cure of his own. It was to distract her from her thoughts and to revive her interest in modern poets that he evidently gave her a copy of Keats's 1817 *Poems*. Her next letter (11th September 1817) is of great interest. It begins gloomily. Her mother, whose ill-health is blamed on her rebellious daughter, suspiciously looks over her shoulder exclaiming "Rubbish! Stuff!" at what she is writing. Nevertheless, "other people's rubbish being as acceptable as anything I could say", she writes of poetry. After quoting at length from Elton's *Specimens of Classic Poets*, she turns to the moderns.

> You cannot think how these [by a contemporary of Sappho] have interested me; so much perhaps because they are not modern.—Yes! though I *would* not *love* Keats' (I do like his verses) I am not quite an insensible. . . . When you are in a humour please write me out Keats' hyacinth; you see I am not prejudiced, for I think very highly of his genius and ability, though I do not admire all his poetry; I am very sincere too, thus to confess my want of taste and——

And—but at that point, this contemporary critique of Keats breaks off for ever. The reason is plain in the scribbled address of the letter—"Mr. John Taylor, Lincoln!!!" As she wrote, John Taylor himself walked into the house on an unexpected visit. We may guess that he was anxious to see how his cure was working: we may be sure that they continued the discussion of Keats and the poem which he had evidently mentioned to her, "Keats' hyacinth".

What was this mysterious poem? Nothing in Keats's works corresponds to such a description. The famous lines from *Fancy*

Shaded hyacinth, alway
Sapphire queen of the mid-May:

were not written until over a year later. Besides, shorter poems written during 1817, the year of the composition of *Endymion*, are naturally rare. A tempting guess, indeed, would be the lines from *Endymion* itself, Book IV, lines 66–69,

O for Hermes' wand
To touch this flower into human shape!
That woodland Hyacinthus could escape
From his green prison,

but this seems improbable. Keats did not finish Book III until September 26th, recording the date on his draft MS., and probably did not start Book IV until October. There is no sign in the MS. that these lines are interpolated from any earlier draft; so, though this last possibility cannot quite be ruled out, it seems that "Keats' hyacinth" was a separate poem, known to Taylor and now lost.

It is tantalising to realise, too, that this poem was nearly preserved for us by Taylor's continued efforts to occupy his cousin's mind. Although Mary Drury did not claim to be a writer herself—a "*dreadful* criticism" of Lady Morgan's *France* in the *Quarterly Review* caused her to exclaim in her next letter "Ye powers, defend *me* from the ambition of becoming Authoress!"—her teaching experience had, in fact, made her ambitious to produce educational books, especially of the anthology kind. Since 1813 she had been asking her brothers, James and John, to print her book of historical quotations, and was now disappointed to see that a rival volume by the Reverend G. Whittaker had just come out; she was also at work on a companion volume of anecdotes from English History. John Taylor evidently thought more highly than her own family of her flair for this work. Knowing her fondness for flower-pieces, he now proposed that she should submit an anthology of literary allusions to flowers with a view to publication, apparently under the editorship of Reynolds. She was delighted, and at once transcribed the whole of her "poetical Flora". In October she is still sending additional pieces, notably Chatterton's lyrics, and finding, as her cousin hoped she would, such "business" a "specific" against "dismals". There can be little doubt that "Keats' hyacinth" was among such pieces, especially as Taylor himself had a hand in the collection, as appears from a later incident; for, although Mary's anthology never saw print, the idea of a "Flora" to be published by Taylor and Hessey was realised six years later, in 1823, when they produced *Flora Domestica* by Elizabeth Kent, Leigh Hunt's sister-in-law. On March 14th, 1823, Hessey wrote to John Taylor about this book

> As for adding to the Poetical illustrations, I scarcely think it worth while unless anything very striking were at hand in your portfolio—You had some passages collected by your Cousin and yourself—if you could find them, and look them over directly it might be easy to put some of them under their proper heads—but there is no end to such additions.*

Taylor was by this time too involved in business to look at anything "directly"; the "portfolio" had vanished; Elizabeth Kent's *Flora Domestica*, though it quotes the lines from *Fancy* under the heading "Hyacinth", is silent on "Keats' hyacinth".

Why did the cousins abandon their anthology, which, to judge by the later success of Elizabeth Kent's collection, might have been a promising venture? The answer lies in Mary Drury's subsequent history, which is also strangely connected with that of Keats. In the next year, 1818, her dismissed lover, James Tallant, returned from America, defied mother and brothers, and claimed her. The event is commented on by Hessey.

> What! More Tallants? I thought there were enough in the family already. . . . There seems a wonderful affinity between the Drurys and the Tallants—I hope the "young folks" will be happy, though it is an unpromising beginning when such a connection is formed in opposition to the will of Parents.

In the following year she joined her husband beyond the

* Hyder E. Rollins, *The Keats Circle*, II, 434.

Atlantic. Hessey's shrewd banter to John Taylor may contain some truth—

> I dare say you will find your visit less pleasing at Lincoln—you were getting rather fond of your cousin were you not?

for Taylor wrote at the beginning of 1820 to Michael Drury in Philadelphia

> I am much concerned to hear of the far-away Wanderings of my dear Cousin your Sister Mary.—The Change since I last saw her, seems more like a Dream than a Reality—*

Now, the bearer of this letter to Michael Drury was none other than George Keats, younger brother of the poet, who had just made his flying visit to England to see his brother and to raise money for his own trading ventures in Louisville, Kentucky. This was the occasion, a few days before the onset of Keats's first hæmorrhage, when, according to several of Keats's friends, Taylor and Hessey among them, George made off with nearly all Keats's remaining capital. That George was innocent of any such intention appears from his later letters, but the sequel is interesting. "The far-away Wanderings" of Mary Tallant and her husband had taken them to settle in Cincinnati. They were therefore within a hundred miles of George Keats and his wife, whom Mary mentioned in her letters to John Taylor, and whom she visited late in 1820 or early in 1821. When Keats was dying at Rome in the winter of 1820–21, Taylor and Hessey advanced him an extra £150. This they tried to extract from George Keats in Louisville by presenting him with a bill for that amount payable to James Tallant at Cincinnati, who was to act as their agent. George refused to acknowledge the debt—though he afterwards paid it through English sources—and the unpaid draft remained in the hands of Mary's husband until 1828, which is the last time we hear of Mr. and Mrs. James Tallant.

Yet it was not to be the last of Cousin Mary. Her postscript, though unconnected with Keats, has a certain pathetic interest of its own. In 1845, John Taylor, now publishing as Taylor and Walton—Hessey having become a schoolmaster—received

* Op. cit. I, 101.

a letter from Mary Edmonds. It was Mary Drury, twice-widowed, but still undefeated, running a girls' day school of twelve to fifteen pupils in the beautiful little Northamptonshire village of Guilsborough. Though the date of James Tallant's death is uncertain, it can be conjectured that she returned from America in 1838; another letter in 1846 speaks of her having, for the first time in eight years, all her four children with her—Julius, John, Sarah and Alice Tallant. To her second husband she owed her connection with Guilsborough, where the Edmonds family had owned property. Her publishing schemes were unabated. She had at last persuaded her brother James to print her grammar book, and her son John is bringing Taylor the MS. of a history book. John is setting out in publishing himself, and, to her great joy, has been offered a post with Taylor and Walton: one can guess once again the kindly influence of her cousin.

Unfortunately, a final letter almost brings an anti-climax. Young John Tallant did not find favour with Mr. Walton; Taylor could not secure him the job. His mother writes in a manner that recalls the impulsive and sensitive Mary Drury of over a quarter of a century before. She remembers "the many misfortunes and injuries heaped upon us by some from whom we had good right to expect otherwise . . ." Her mother, her brothers, or her husbands? One does not know, but "this failure is only one more of the many disappointing results which have overtaken me in the course of my ever-varying and much-afflicted life". Yet, she consoles herself, John is a good son, and she is happy in her daughters, her school, her house and her neighbours. Indeed, these consolations were not in vain. John prospered and, in the end, published on his own account several school-books by his mother; the girls, Sarah and Alice, grew old with her, "the Misses Tallant", helping their mother to make the little school one of the most respected in the neighbourhood; and there is living today a nonagenarian who remembers receiving, at the age of five, his first writing lesson at the Guilsborough school from an old lady. She taught him to write the letter M, her own initial—Mary Drury, Cousin Mary, the one authority we have for Keats's *Hyacinth*.*

* Taylor MSS. at Bakewell, Derbyshire. All quotations, unless otherwise indicated, are taken from these, by kind permission of H. C. Brooke-Taylor, Esq.

10

"THE CAP AND BELLS"

To Edmund Blunden

I

CRITICS and biographers have found little good to say about the last work of Keats's life, the long unfinished poem entitled *The Cap and Bells* or *The Jealousies*. "Unfortunate", "rubbish", "strained frivolities" are some of Sir Sidney Colvin's remarks. Miss Hewlett speaks of its "confusion of theme". There is a tendency to blame these poor qualities on his friend, Charles Brown, since it was, according to the latter, a conversation between the two men which led to the poem. Colvin even speaks of the poem as if it were in some way a collaboration with Brown, like their ill-fated play *Otho the Great*. Brown, indeed, claimed that he "knew all" about the poem, and "was to assist" in one part of it; but there is no evidence that he ever did, and his own note, appended to the first printed version in 1848, seems to contradict the knowledge which he claimed:

> This Poem was written subject to future amendments and omissions: it was begun without a plan, and without any prescribed laws for the supernatural machinery.

He also spoke of the poem as being written "chiefly for amusement."

The chief trouble seems to be that no one can say clearly what the poem is about. Brown who "knew all" is completely silent on this point, merely remarking cryptically that "it appeared to be a relaxation". Leigh Hunt, who published some stanzas from it during the poet's lifetime, does not speak of it in his own autobiography. Keats's only recorded comment on the poem was "If ever I come to publish . . . there will be some delicate pickings for squeamish stomachs", which suggests a far more savage and robust satire than the poem appears to be, but still leaves its main purpose in obscurity. An interesting remark by Lord Jeffrey, immediately after the publication in 1848, speaks of the poem as "more suited to an Italian than an English taste", but leaves us equally in doubt whether he saw any precise meaning in it.

Later critics have been almost as vague. The poem is thought to be a satire, in the style of Byron, on "the unedifying matrimonial and love affairs of the Prince Regent". It has also been suggested that Keats, as well as taking Byron's style, took him as a subject for his satire, and that it is *his* love-affairs with which the poem deals. Certainly no one has been able to take the parallel with the Prince Regent very far, and a careful survey of the poem shows that of the whole 88 stanzas of the poem, only these (stanzas XVII and XVIII) point at all at the future George IV:

> 'I'll trounce 'em!—there's the square-cut chancellor,
> His son shall never touch that bishopric;
> And for the nephew of old Palfior,
> I'll show him that his speeches made me sick,
> And give the colonelcy to Phalaric;
> The tiptoe marquis, moral and gallant,
> Shall lodge in shabby taverns upon tick;
> And for the Speaker's second cousin's aunt,
> She sha'n't be maid of honour,—by heaven that she sha'n't!'
>
> 'I'll shirk the Duke of A.; I'll cut his brother;
> I'll give no garter to his eldest son;
> I won't speak to his sister or his mother!
> The Viscount B. shall live at cut-and-run;
> But how in the world can I contrive to stun
> That fellow's voice, which plagues me worse than any,
> That stubborn fool, that impudent state-dun,
> Who sets down ev'ry sovereign as a zany,—
> That vulgar commoner, Esquire Biancopany?'

These stanzas might be taken to represent the irritation felt by the Prince Regent at the members of Parliament, who so often criticised him, especially "Biancopany", a transparent Italianism for Whitbread—Samuel Whitbread, who consistently, till his death in 1815, opposed the Regency and championed the Princess of Wales. As far as the whole poem goes, there is, however, a peculiarity about these two stanzas, which Charles Brown incidentally characterised as among the examples of "failures in wit" in the poem. An examination of the numbering of the stanzas in Keats's original MS. reveals, in Dr. Garrod's words, "that stanzas XVII—XVIII are an afterthought or subsequent insertion" by Keats. If the only stanzas directly concerned with the Prince Regent were an afterthought on Keats's part, it is unlikely that the main theme of the poem, as first conceived, could be this topical subject, especially as it is one which Keats nowhere mentions in his letters, though other political events are frequently glanced at. In fact, his only mention of the Prince Regent, in the summer of 1819, is one of indifference:

> I can pass a summer very quietly without caring much about Fat Louis, fat Regent or the Duke of Wellington.

All this suggests that, instead of trying to make the poem conform as a commentary on topical and political events, we should try to examine how it fits in with Keats's own life—when and in what circumstances it was written; for if the clue eluded even his friends, it is likely to be some more personal matter. It will not do merely to dismiss the work as evidence of failing powers. It contains many stanzas which his friends then and readers now have recognised as characteristic and beautiful. Nor can it be explained simply as nonsense poetry. Clearly it meant something to Keats; however loosely he planned its structure, he would never have contemplated publishing for a general public something that was merely a private whimsy, an exercise in light verse. The number of times he mentions the poem in his letters shows that it was in some way bound up with his life: his life, at the time he was writing it, may provide the clue, and fortunately the facts of his life at this time are fairly plain.

Keats's brief reference to "fat Regent" was written to his sister Fanny from Winchester on Saturday, August 28th, 1819. He was approaching a crisis in his life. His poems had not been successful, and money was short. He had an "understanding", in the nature of a secret engagement, with his

Hampstead neighbour, Fanny Brawne. A fortnight later, the crisis was precipitated by a letter which arrived from Keats's brother, George, in America. George had lost his existing capital in a trading venture, and was ruined unless Keats could raise more money for him. After a visit to London to do this, Keats returned to Winchester in an unsettled state, although on Sunday, September 19th, he managed to write the serene *Ode to Autumn.* By the night of Tuesday, September 21st, his mind was made up. He wrote to several friends on this and succeeding dates. The burden of these letters is all the same. He will "no longer live upon hopes", either of his poems or of his recently completed play. He now intended to earn a living by literary journalism, dwelling for this purpose not at Hampstead, but in some place nearer Fleet Street, Bloomsbury, and the haunts of journalism. He felt confident that the most successful literary journalist of his acquaintance, William Hazlitt, would help him in this project. "I shall enquire of Hazlitt how the figures of the market stand," he wrote, and again, "I shall apply to Hazlitt, who knows the market as well as anyone, for something to bring me in a few pounds as soon as possible." Another friend, Charles Wentworth Dilke, obtained him lodgings at 25 College Street, Westminster, and Keats returned to London early in October.

This journalistic plan broke down almost before it had started. A visit to Fanny Brawne with Charles Brown completely destroyed Keats's resolve. He poured out a number of swiftly-written poems to her, became, it seems, officially engaged, and returned to Hampstead to live next door to her. For three agitated and unhappy months, he did nothing but revise his poems, for a forthcoming book, and the play, rejected by one management, for consideration by another. Much of his time was also spent on financial and legal business in the City on George's behalf. Early in the New Year, George suddenly appeared himself from America, leaving again at the end of January with, so Charles Brown said, not only his own available capital but that of Keats as well. A few days afterwards Keats had the hæmorrhage which announced the end of his writing career, and foretold the end of life itself just over a year later.

Against this background, Brown places fairly clearly the

composition of *The Cap and Bells*. It was written, he says, in the mornings at Wentworth Place, Hampstead, and therefore was begun after Keats returned to that address in mid-October, 1819. Brown refers rather mysteriously to the breaking-off of the poem. "This morning . . . employment was broken into by a circumstance which it is needless to mention. He could not resume that employment, and he became dreadfully unhappy. His hopes of fame, and other more tender hopes were blighted." This utterance by Brown, which Sir Sidney Colvin calls "oracular", has never been thoroughly examined; if anything, it has been thought loosely to refer to the agitation and jealousy which Keats felt over his engagement to Fanny. This, however, is not at all the way in which Brown generally refers to her; besides, it is the engagement which is referred to as "other more tender hopes". Now, at the time Brown wrote these words in his Memoir of Keats, he made it clear that he still regarded George Keats as culpable for his brother's unhappiness and even for his death. Commenting on this, he adds "But I am sliding off into a subject, *from which I chose to refrain in the Memoir*." It seems certain that the "circumstance which it is needless to mention" and the "subject, from which I chose to refrain" are one and the same—George's arrival from America, importunate for money. Indeed, in a letter of January 15th, 1820, to his sister-in-law, Keats showed himself a little put out by George's cavalier treatment of him on his visit, though he may not have uttered the reproachful words about money-matters that Brown has recorded. At all events, this gives a fairly certain date for the breaking-off of *The Cap and Bells*, that is, about the middle of January 1820, the poem apparently having been on the go for about three months on and off.

This dating is confirmed by the internal evidence of the poem itself and of Keats's letters. As Lord Jeffrey said, the poem is Italianate in style. It resembles in particular the style of Ariosto, whom Keats had been reading that autumn at Winchester, and continued to read on his return to Hampstead. The connection with Ariosto links, in a curious way, with another work which Keats was reading far more consistently in the autumn of 1819, and, indeed, had been reading steadily throughout the year. This was Burton's *The Anatomy of Melancholy*, a long paragraph of which he had copied out for his brother George in September, and whose influence is to be seen in the poems he wrote to Fanny Brawne in October. Burton, on the subject of jealousy, actually quotes Ariosto:

> This is that cruel wound against whose smart,
> No liquors force prevailes, nor any plaister,
> No skill of starres, no depth of magick art,
> Devised by that great clerk Zoroaster;

Now Keats not only chose, as a sub-title for his poem, the name *The Jealousies*, but preferred it as a title to *The Cap and Bells*. Moreover, the second stanza of his poem begins:

> This was a crime forbidden by the law;
> And all the priesthood of his city wept,
> For ruin and dismay they well foresaw,
> If impious prince no bound or limit kept,
> And faery Zendervester overstept;

Zend-Avesta is the original document of the religion of Zoroaster, the Parsee Bible. There could be no possible reason for Keats to use the word unless he had the stanza of Ariosto in mind, and, always being strongly affected by anything he met in quotation, he almost certainly got it from Burton. The arrangement of Burton's work in sections and subsections is also echoed in Keats's poem by the line

> (Section'd and subsection'd with learning sage,)

while unusual words in the poem, such as "Cham" and "Janizaries" were taken from Burton's chapters on Religious Melancholy and were marked by Keats in his copy of the work.

It is clear that Keats started to write the poem in the middle of October 1819, when he was reading both Ariosto and Burton. It seems likely that by the time of George's visit three months later, in the middle of January 1820, he had completed, and probably copied for George, about eighty or so stanzas. Whether he had written the whole poem as we know it, or whether he struggled through a few more stanzas after he became seriously ill, we shall never know. That he had got so far, and that the poem was fresh in his mind on January 28th, 1820 (the day of George's departure for America), seems indicated by a letter he wrote to his sister-in-law on that day. In this, in quick succession, he mentions Moore's Almanack, a sampler, and a kettle-drum. These unlikely ingredients are found in stanzas 56, 49 and 78 respectively of the poem. He also had said, a month before, "I shall be very busy . . . and shall be for some time, in preparing some poems to come out in the Spring." These were, of course, the volume of *Lamia, The Eve of St. Agnes* and other poems, eventually published in June, 1820, and he was evidently working on these during the month of January, as well as copying some of them, particularly the *Ode to a Nightingale*, for George. The later stanzas of *The Cap and Bells* contain many distinct echoes of these poems, especially of *The Eve of St. Agnes* and of *Hyperion*. The last of these echoes is the last couplet of stanza 82 of the poem, whose

> As when the sea, at flow, gluts up once more
> The craggy hollowness of a wild-reefed shore.

exactly recalls the image from *Hyperion*

> like sullen waves
> In the half-glutted hollows of reef-rocks

Indeed, the likenesses between *Hyperion* and some of these later stanzas are so great that one may believe that he was deliberately using images from the epic to fill out the comic poem. According to his publishers, he regarded *Hyperion* as unfinished, and did not finally wish them to publish it, and he may have been treating it in the same way as he treated the unfinished and unpublished *Eve of St. Mark*, ideas from which are also incorporated in *The Cap and Bells*. At all events, the evidence of these later stanzas shows that most, if not all that we have of *The Cap and Bells* had been written by Keats between the middle of October 1819 and the middle of January 1820. It remains to be seen what we can make of the poem written in these months of stress.

II

Stripped of extraneous detail, the story of the poem, so far as it goes, is simple. Elfinan, fairy Emperor, is in love with a mortal named Bertha Pearl, but to please his people is betrothed to a fairy princess, Bellanaine, daughter of Pigmio of Imaus, who is herself in love with a mortal named Hubert. His Chancellor, Crafticanto, leaves Panthea, capital of Elfinan's Empire, to fetch the princess; meanwhile Elfinan, dreading his marriage, summons his dark slave, Eban, to fetch the magician Hum, who is in the town. Hum, an engaging rascal, arrives at the palace and, while consuming a great deal of drink, supplies Elfinan with a magic book, which, he assures him, will enable him to carry off Bertha Pearl. Elfinan leaves for Bertha's home, Canterbury, just as Crafticanto's embassy returns, escorting the princess and her maid Coralline. After a digression, giving Crafticanto's diary of the journey, they enter the palace, to find Elfinan gone, and everything in confusion. Crafticanto discovers Hum, drunk, and at that point the poem breaks off.

One thing at once emerges from the rather confused scene-setting of the poem. Panthea is London, a large capital city with northern suburbs, already beginning to be lit by gas, and in which the transport is by hackney coach. The characters, however, apart from the hoarse-voiced Cockney coachman, are all fairies. Bertha and Hubert never appear. Who are these elfin inhabitants meant to be? The answer may be found in what had been Keats's original intention of how he was going to spend his time in London that winter. He intended, as has been seen, to devote himself to literary journalism, to enter into the cockpit, as he called it, of contemporary periodical work, and to learn his way about this from William Hazlitt, "who knows the market". Hazlitt appears often in Keats's letters. Usually, it is as a writer of superb invective: "he is your only good damner". Keats was moved to quote instances of this "damning" at length in letters to George. On the other hand, he also shows in his letters a knowledge of another aspect of Hazlitt—the shy, saturnine, moody creature, who stared at the floor and could hardly be got to utter a word in company. Keats had satirised this side of Hazlitt in an imaginery dialogue where the essayist appears at a party with the voluble Leigh Hunt and other friends, and, to all their remarks, only answers "Yes, sir", "No, sir".

Now, among the confusions of the poem, one might at first sight include the apparent inconsistencies in the character of

Eban, Elfinan's dusky slave. He is described as "wise, slow, His speech, his only words were 'yes' and 'no' ", yet when he takes a coach to fetch Hum, he pours out upon the driver a flood of invective, lasting for three stanzas, in exactly the style of unflattering description, piling up detail upon detail, which Hazlitt uses in his attacks upon Southey, Gifford, and other literary figures.

> 'I'll pull the string,' said he, and further said,
> 'Polluted jarvey! Ah, thou filthy hack!
> Whose springs of life are all dried up and dead,
> Whose linsey-wolsey lining hangs all slack,
> Whose rug is straw, whose wholeness is a crack;
> And evermore thy steps go clatter-clitter;
> Whose glass once up can never be got back,
> Who prov'st, with jolting arguments and bitter,
> That 'tis of modern use to travel in a litter.'
>
> 'Thou inconvenience! thou hungry crop
> For all corn! thou snail-creeper to and fro,
> Who while thou goest ever seem'st to stop,
> And fiddle-faddle standest while you go;
> I' the morning, freighted with a weight of woe;
> Unto some lazar-house thou journeyest,
> And in the evening tak'st a double row
> Of dowdies, for some dance or party drest,
> Besides the goods meanwhile thou movest east and west.'
>
> 'By thy ungallant bearing and sad mien,
> An inch appears the utmost thou couldst budge;
> Yet at the slightest nod, or hint, or sign,
> Round to the curb-stone patient dost thou trudge,
> School'd in a beckon, learned in a nudge,
> A dull-eyed Argus watching for a fare;
> Quiet and plodding thou dost bear no grudge
> To whisking tilburies, or phaetons rare,
> Curricles, or mail-coaches, swift beyond compare.'

This is precisely in the style of Hazlitt's attack on Gifford, quoted earlier in the year by Keats—"your invincible pertness, your mercenary malice, your impenetrable dullness, your bare-faced impudence, your pragmatical self-sufficiency, your hypocritical zeal, your pious frauds . . ." and so on.

The likeness between the two sides of Hazlitt's character and the two aspects of Eban might conceivably be a coincidence, if it were not for the physical description of both characters. Eban is the only person in the poem whose appearance and manner is portrayed with any care. He is dark, "swift of look, and foot", and his hair is long, wavy, and black; in a cancelled stanza

> Past either Ear half shown, his plenteous hair
> Went in a jetty wreath, and on his back
> Met in curl clusters

Above all, he takes every opportunity quietly to study his own appearance

> He smiled at self, and, smiling, show'd his teeth,
> And seeing his white teeth, he smiled the more;
> Lifted his eye-brows, spurn'd the path beneath,
> Show'd teeth again, and smiled as heretofore,
> Until he knock'd at the magician's door;
> Where, till the porter answer'd, might be seen,
> In the clear panel more he could adore,——

Now with Hazlitt, according to Bryan Waller Procter

> . . . there was something in his earnest, irritable face, his restless eye, his black hair, combed backwards and curling (not too resolutely) about a well-shaped head that was very striking . . . he had a quick restless eye . . . he always presented a very clean and neat appearance when he went abroad.

Then, even more strikingly, there is this description of his habits, from Haydon's *Autobiography*:

> One day I called on him and found him arranging his hair before a glass, trying different effects, and asking my advice whether he should show his forehead more or less. In that large wainscotted room Milton had conceived, and perhaps written, many of his finest thoughts, and there sat one of his critics admiring his own features.

These detailed descriptions coincide so well that, taken with the other coincidences of manner and speech, they can lead to only one conclusion. Eban the slave in *The Cap and Bells* is a portrait of Hazlitt the essayist, the man whom Keats took as an authority for the life of literary journalism he had intended to lead. In that association, we may perhaps see the clue to the intention of the whole poem.

III

The question is whether this picture of Hazlitt is an integral part of the poem, or whether it was a caprice on Keats's part. Eban disappears from the poem at stanza 40; in the scheme of things, so far as it can be gathered, he does not seem likely to have returned. His place, particularly in strength and detail of characterisation, is taken by the mercurial charlatan Hum, and it is to Hum that we should next turn for a hint of what the poem is meant to be about.

Hum is a likeable rogue with various eccentricities which appear in the poem. His first appearance, however, is in a stanza which Keats cancelled, and, with the picture of Eban as Hazlitt in mind, it is an extremely significant one. For Hum appears, in Eban's words, as a literary man in the centre of a fashionable literary circle.

> 'Ho! Ho!' thought Eban, 'so this Signor Hum
> A Conversazione holds tonight
> Whene'er he beats his literary drum
> The learned muster round all light and tight
> Drest in best black to talk by candlelight.'
> E'en while he thought, for eighteen penny fare
> He paid a half penny by cunning sleight
> Made argent; then with self-contented Air
> Broke through the crowd to Hums and all the world was there.

There is, of course, one distinct literary figure whom this description fits like a glove, as clearly, indeed, as his own name chimes with that Hum. This is Leigh Hunt. His type of literary conversazione was well-known to Keats. It was a scene such as this that Keats had parodied earlier this year, when he described the literary party at which Hazlitt had only been able to say "Yes, sir, no, sir". Hunt was obsessed with all things Italian, like our modern Francophiles with all things French. He spoke, sang and quoted Italian; he addressed Keats as "Giovanni mio". None of Keats's friends could better be described as "Signor Hum". Moreover, his reputation was at a low ebb with Keats at this very moment, and that of his literary parties. Keats wrote on January 15th, 1820, "Almost all the parties I may chance to fall into I know by heart. . . . If I go to Hunt's I run my head into many times heard puns and music." There is no doubt that Keats's long-standing irritation is vented in the stanza on Signor Hum.

Yet it must be remembered that Keats cancelled this stanza. Granted his intention to parody Hunt as Hum, did he continue with it, or did he, remembering their original friendship and Hunt's real kindness, abandon it? Some of Hum's habits and doings must now be considered, in the order in which the poem shows them. We are first told, by his servant, that Hum is in financial difficulties. He then enters, walking downstairs backwards, a habit of his. He runs with Eban to the palace where they find the Emperor playing on a mysterious instrument called a Man-Tiger-Organ, which they hear through the door of his room. This causes them great fear, and they enter prostrating themselves. Eban is dismissed, and Hum proceeds to advise the Emperor in his love-affair, and produces the magic book. They see Crafticanto's embassy returning with the Princess, and Hum describes it poetically, and reveals that he writes poetry. All this while Hum has been drinking, and he is eventually found by Crafticanto "far gone in liquor".

To begin with, Leigh Hunt was at this exact time in financial difficulty. He had even been briefly arrested for debt. "Hunt was arrested the other day. He soon however dated from his own house again." The phantasy of walking downstairs backwards may be left for the moment, but there is an even more fantastic connection between Leigh Hunt and the curiously-named Man-Tiger-Organ, which he hears through the door of Elfinan's room.

In Leigh Hunt's *Autobiography* there is a fascinating section on childhood fears. He speaks of the terror of certain pictures, a horror accentuated by the teasing of his elder brother:

There was a fabulous wild beast, a portrait of which, in

> some picture-book, unspeakably shocked me. It was called the Mantichora. It had the head of a man, grinning with rows of teeth, and the body of a wild beast, brandishing a tail armed with stings. It was sometimes called by the ancients *Mar*tichora. But I did not know that. I took the word to be a horrible compound of *man* and *tiger* . . . . . My brother played me repeated tricks with this frightful anomaly. I was always ready to be frightened again. At one time he would grin like the Mantichora; then he would roar like him; then call about him in the dark. I remember his asking me to come up to him one night at the top of the house. I ascended, and found the door shut. Suddenly a voice came through the key-hole, saying, in its hollowest tones, "The Mantichora's coming." Down I rushed to the parlour, fancying the terror at my heels.

There is little doubt that this childhood fear, which Hunt may have communicated in one of his voluble outpourings to Keats, has much to do with Hum's fear and the curious introduction of the Man-Tiger-Organ into the poem. Hum, chatty, cheeky, never at a loss, talks on with Elfinan quite in the style of Hunt. The likeness is most clear when he turns poetical.

> 'Wounds! How they shout!' said Hum, 'and there,—
> see, see!
> Th' Ambassador's return'd from Pigmio!
> The morning's very fine—uncommonly!
> See, past the skirts of yon white cloud they go,
> Tinging it with soft crimsons! Now below
> The sable-pointed heads of firs and pines
> They dip, move on, and with them moves a glow
> Along the forest side! Now amber lines
> Reach the hill top, and now throughout the valley shines.'
>
> 'Why, Hum, you're getting quite poetical!
> Those *nows* you managed in a special style.'
> 'If ever you have leisure, sire, you shall
> See scraps of mine will make it worth your while,
> Tit-bits for Phoebus!'

"Those *nows* you managed in a special style"—Keats was thoroughly conversant with, and indeed had been influenced himself by the "special style" of Hunt's poetry. Hunt's best-known work to date was *The Story of Rimini*, a re-telling of the love-story of Paolo and Francesca, expanding the fifth canto of Dante's *Inferno*, where the lovers appear in one of the world's most moving passages. Poor Hunt succeeded in producing some ludicrous effects in this poem, by a mixture of naïvety and over-confidence; but he was certainly read and quoted, sometimes even with approval, by his young disciple. Hunt, incidentally, had a mock-modest way of referring to his work, much in the style of Hum's "Tit-bits for Phoebus!" Keats makes him say of his work at the parodied party, "O we are spinning on a little". What the "special style" of this work was like may be seen from the main scene of the first canto of *The Story of Rimini*, where Francesca is waiting for the wedding-embassy to arrive.

> The talk increases now, and now advance,
> Space after space, with many a sprightly prance,
> The pages of the court, in rows of three;
> Of white and crimson is their livery.
> Space after space,—and yet the attendants come,—
> And deeper goes about the impatient hum—
> Ah—yes—no—'tis not he—but 'tis the squires
> Who go before him when his pomp requires;
> And now his huntsman shows the lessening train,
> Now the squire-carver, and the chamberlain,—
> And now his banner comes, and now his shield
> Borne by the squire that waits him to the field,—
> And then an interval,—a lordly space;—
> A pin-drop silence strikes o'er all the place;
> The princess, from a distance, scarcely knows
> Which way to look; her colour comes and goes;
> And with an impulse and affection free
> She lays her hand upon her father's knee,
> Who looks upon her with a laboured smile,
> Gathering it up into his own the while,
> When some one's voice, as if it know not how
> To check itself, exclaims, 'the prince! now—now!'

It can hardly be doubted, after this extract, that Hunt, like Hum, manages his Nows "in a special style". It is, in fact, the typical weakness of his poetry that he strings together these loosely-connected lists of images, a fault which the harsh critics of *Endymion* also saw imitated in that poem by Keats. By the winter of 1819–20, Keats had grown beyond *Endymion*; he had grown beyond Hunt—except to parody him, his ingratiating manners, and even his poetry in the character of the magician Hum.

There is one objection that may be raised against this identification of Hunt with Hum. When Keats was seriously ill six months later in the summer of 1820, he went to lodge near Hunt in Kentish Town, and, as his illness increased, even went to stay with the Hunts, for the sake of company and nursing. The Hunts were kindly if feckless, and Keats could never be seriously out of humour with Hunt once he was within the circle of his considerable and genuine charm—in that respect his character as Hum the magician may be thought particularly appropriate. Keats took his MS. of the unfinished *Cap and Bells* to Kentish Town, intending to re-start it; indeed, it is just possible that the last half-dozen stanzas of the fragment, which show a completely different turn to the story, together with a lack of poetic invention, were added at this time. He had it with him at Hunt's own house, and when he left in a hurry, after an unfortunate misunder-standing, due as much to his own illness as to any fault of his host, he asked Hunt to send the MS. after him. It is to be wondered if he would carry with him, work on, or still more, leave about a poem which satirised, however obscurely, his friend. Yet we do not know which parts of the poem Keats showed Hunt, apart from the three 'coachman' stanzas. Nor, even though, as Charles Brown said, the poem was written largely for amusement, was it a poem that could afford to be too obvious to its victims; this, in fact, may be the very cause of some of its obscurity, that the clues were deliberately shuffled.

Certainly something of this sort seems to have happened here. Hum contains two characteristics which would blind Hunt to the likeness to himself. One is the fantastic habit, attributed to Hum, of coming downstairs backwards. Hunt is frank to the point of being a little tedious in writing about his own foibles, but nothing resembles this in his autobiography. The other is that Hum constantly tipples. Hunt's excesses ran on the lines of extravagance and sex; but his worst enemies never suggested that he was a drunkard. These two notes, however, chime curiously with another literary figure. Hum's first idiosyncrasy is described thus in the poem:

> 'He always comes down backward, with one shoe'—
> Return'd the porter—'off, and one shoe on,
> Like, saving shoe for sock or stocking, my man John!'

It may be remembered that Charles Lamb, at the "immortal dinner" of B. R. Haydon's, at which Keats was present, had insulted a Civil Service acquaintance of Wordsworth by singing at him

> Diddle iddle don
> My son John
> Went to bed with his breeches on,
> One stocking off and one stocking on,
> My son John!

Lamb was tipsy; it was a state he was often in, and this may well have been his song when he was. Hum—the name a combination of Hunt and Lamb—surely carries a trace of the latter. Three parts of Hunt to one of Lamb is the recipe for the not unlikeable Hum.

IV

One must now ask again what the poem is about. Its characters, at all events these subsidiary ones, seem to be emerging, somewhat surprisingly, as literary figures of Keats's day. Yet this is not, in fact, so surprising when we remember how Keats had originally planned to spend this autumn and winter, in the pursuit of topical, literary journalism. His plans had broken down under the stress of his impetuous love; but Keats was, for all his "chameleon poet" vagaries, very tenacious of an idea once he had conceived it. Here was his outlet for the course his personal life had compelled him to divert—to write, in verse, and in the disguise of a fairy-tale, a satire on the literary figures of his day. He was in a mood to satirise the London literary society in which he moved, as appears again most strongly in his letter to his sister-in-law. "Upon the whole

I dislike Mankind. . . . I know the different Styles of talk in different places: what subjects will be started how it will proceed, like an acted play, from the first to the last, Act. . . . All I can say is that standing at Charing cross and looking east west north and South I can see nothing but dullness." This mood of gloomy irritation, due partly to his failing health, had been on him all autumn. He was in a mood to spy out the faults in his contemporaries.

In this connection, his taste among his fellow-writers is interesting. He had given it, humorously but sincerely, earlier in 1819, when he described himself as one who does "not admire . . . Tom Moore, Rob Southey and Mr Rogers; and does admire W^m^. Hazlitt . . . half of Wordsworth, and none of Crabbe." This is an accurate survey of his taste, for he elaborated his "half of Wordsworth" idea a month later, in a review of his friend Reynolds's devastating parody of Wordsworth's *Peter Bell*. If *The Cap and Bells* is a literary satire, one must expect to find some of the major dislikes on Keats's list in it. Now, the least sympathetic character in the poem is Elfinan's Chancellor, Crafticanto. He is presented as elderly, sly, prying, hypocritical, censorious, self-satisfied and prosy, though aware that he is considered all these things.

> (I've got a conscience, maugre people's jokes)

Above all he appears, for all his self-satisfied shrewdness, as a master of the obvious.

> Show him a mouse's tail, and he will guess,
> With metaphysic swiftness, at the mouse;
> Show him a garden, and with speed no less,
> He'll surmise sagely of a dwelling house.

Now, Crafticanto's name alone suggests one eminent literary figure of whom these lines might be written—Crafty (as Keats first wrote) Canto—Words Worth. Jokes were rife in that punning age about how much his words were worth, how worthy his words were, and so on, and these not only among the poet's detractors, but among his friends such as Charles Lamb. Moreover, the description of the obviousness of much of his verse fits exactly that "half of Wordsworth" which Keats disliked, the "coarse Sampler", in Keats's phrase, of some of his over-simplified rural stories, such as *Peter Bell* itself. Reynolds's parody had pointed this cruelly, in a prose note on the poem purporting to come from Wordsworth himself. As well as mock-obvious lines such as

> On Sunday he is us'd to pray
> In winter he is very cold

Reynolds makes Wordsworth explain the processes of his thought in a preface—

> It has been my aim and my achievement to deduce moral thunder from buttercups, daisies, celandines, and (as a poet, scarcely inferior to myself, hath it) "such small deer." Out of sparrows' eggs I have hatched great truths, and with sextons' barrows have I wheeled into human hearts, piles of the weightiest philosophy.

The poet "scarcely inferior to myself" is, of course, Shakespeare with his "rats and mice and such small deer". All this is precisely the tone of

> Show him a mouse's tail, and he will guess
> With metaphysic swiftness, at the mouse;

It must be remembered that Keats had read this parody only six months before *The Cap and Bells*; yet it was only "half of Wordsworth" that Keats disliked, and it is obvious that Crafticanto is not a full-length portrait of this particular Lake poet. It does, however, lead one to think of another writer in that school, and a letter of Robert Southey, written again in this same year of 1819, where he too expresses his opinion of modern poetry, his own, and Wordsworth's.

> The swarm of imitative poets in this age is really surprising, and the success with which they imitate their models would be surprising also, if it did not prove that there can be no great difficulty in procuring what may be imitated so well. Morbid feelings, atrocious principles, exaggerated characters, and instances of monstrous and exaggerated horror, make up the fashionable compound; the more un-English,

> un-Christian, and immoral the better, provided it be slavered over with a froth of philosophy. I have fewer imitators than any other poet of any notoriety; the reason is, that I am less fashionable; and, perhaps also, that I am less a mannerist. To make up for this, I am favoured with more abuse than all the rest collectively. Wordsworth comes in for a very large share, and very often we go together. If my name be found in such company hereafter, it will be enough.

This, again, is directly in the style of Crafticanto, who, in the poem, begins his memoirs

> Where, after a long hypocritic howl
> Against the vicious manners of the age
> He goes on to expose, with heart and soul,
> What vice in this or that year was the rage,
> Backbiting all the world in ev'ry page;

Robert Southey, Poet Laureate, and therefore analogous to Crafticanto as Chancellor of Elfinan's Kingdom, was at this time condemned by Keats's set as a one-time revolutionary and radical who had now turned Tory reviewer. The stricture was not altogether just, but Southey, like Crafticanto, had an uneasy conscience about it. He himself confessed that, on occasion, his pen was "dipped in gall". Hence his violence, both in this letter (to a congenial listener, Walter Savage Landor) and in another, written a year later, in which he defended his change of heart bitterly to Shelley, who had attacked him for it. As he says, his name was always linked, and was to be most notably by Byron in a few months' time, with that of Wordsworth. Keats would be following an easily-recognisable and popular pattern in making Crafticanto a combination of Wordsworth and Southey.

His likeness to the latter is seen in the long digression where an extract is given from the memoirs of Crafticanto, dealing with the return of his embassy bringing the Princess to Panthea. To start with, he is characterised as immensely long-winded in his works—"tenth book and chapter nine", the extract starts. Southey was similarly satirised by Byron for his volubility in output:

> He had written much blank verse, and blanker prose,
> And more of both than anybody knows.

Keats, indeed, introduces Crafticanto's diary of the journey quite in the manner of Byron, with a sarcastic apostrophe to Pegasus:

> O, little faery Pegasus! rear—prance—
> Trot round the quarto—ordinary time!
> March, little Pegasus, with pawing hoof sublime.

The sarcastic "little Pegasus" at once recalls the lines of Southey quoted satirically by Byron in the last stanza of the first canto of *Don Juan*

> Go, little book, from this my solitude!
> I cast thee on the waters—go thy ways!
> And if, as I believe, thy vein be good,
> The world will find thee after many days.

and Byron's advice, earlier in the same canto:

> Thou shalt not covet Mr. Southey's Muse,
> His Pegasus, nor anything that's his;

It is indeed Crafticanto's diary, thus introduced, that provides the most convincing likeness between him and the Lake poet. For the diary is a record of an aerial journey over central Asia. The fairy cavalcade, led by the grey-winged Chancellor (Southey's grey hairs had been bandied about in the personalities of literary controversy), flies successfully past Tibet, over the desert of Gobi and a huge volcano in eruption, past a burning city and over an oriental scene of dancing: it is threatened in turn by a shooting star and by a fabulous beast, a griffin. Now Southey's best-known and characteristic poems, *Thalaba* and *The Curse of Kehama*, both have a fantastic oriental setting, and both contain long, mysterious, aerial journeys over Asiatic landscapes full of such portentous properties. The Ship of Heaven, in the latter poem, carries its legendary characters on such a journey as that of Crafticanto's with Bellanaine. It "sails up the fields of ether like an Angel" to land eventually on the peak of the sacred Mount Meru. The images of Southey's poems are huge and exaggerated. Thunderbolts and abysses are commonplaces. His characters are snatched up to the skies, or return, even more precipitately, to earth.

> Through the red sky terrific meteors scour:
> Huge stones come hailing down: or sulphur shower,
> Floating amid the lurid air like snow.

Keats, nevertheless, does not seem to be merely parodying the absurder aspects of Southey's epics. It looks as if he was also trying to emulate the fashion for such epics by taking the good of Southey, when it came, into his own poem. The following stanza by Keats has often been quoted to show how *The Cap and Bells*, in spite of its general unsatisfactory quality, also contains passages of poetic beauty.

> As flowers turn their faces to the sun,
> So on our flight with hungry eyes they gaze,
> And, as we shaped our course, this, that way run,
> With mad-cap pleasure or hand-clasp'd amaze;
> Sweet in the air a mild-toned music plays,
> And progresses through its own labyrinth;
> Buds gather'd from the green spring's middle-days,
> They scatter'd,—daisy, primrose, hyacinth,—
> Or round white columns wreath'd from capital to plinth.

It has not been observed how this resembles the occasional natural felicities of description that break into Southey's turgid oriental scenes, such as this from *Thalaba*:

> But oh the joy! The blessed sight!
> When in that burning waste the Travellers
> Saw a green meadow, fair with flowers besprent,
> Azure and yellow, like the beautiful fields
> Of England, when amid the growing grass
> The blue-bell bends, the golden king-cup shines,
> And the sweet cowslip scents the genial air,
> In the merry month of May!

Keats's satire, or the intention of it, now is fairly clear. If Crafticanto is Southey with a dash of Wordsworth, and Hum is

Hunt with a dash of Lamb, it resolves itself into a battle of the poets of his time, roughly the Lake School versus the "Cockney" which was to crystallise only a few years later in Lamb's famous "Letter from Elia to Robert Southey", the main object of which was to defend not so much himself but Leigh Hunt from Southey's strictures. It is clear that Crafticanto and Hum are on opposite sides in the politics of Panthea. "That vile imposter Hum——" is Crafticanto's description of his rival, while Hum displays a disrespectful attitude toward the authority of the Chancellor. Just as Byron had grouped his poets in the first canto of *Don Juan*, so Keats, with less clarity, was trying to pin down the factions in the kingdom of contemporary poetry.

V

If Panthea is the capital of Poetry, then who is its Emperor, Elfinan? The obvious answer has indeed been given before, and may be at least partly accepted. It is Lord Byron. His position—he had been in exile for three years—his notoriety, his independence from other writers, his aristocratic temper, made him a kind of literary king—indeed, Keats had called him that in a letter just a year earlier. His recent publication of the first two cantos of *Don Juan*—"Lord Byron's last flash poem" as Keats called it—had brought him to the forefront of the public mind: This "superfine rich or noble" poet—again to quote Keats in a satirical mood—stood in everyone's opinion, whether they liked his work or not, as a leader of literature; he "had a demon" as Hazlitt said. At the same time, Keats was always on his guard against his superficial attractions—"Lord Byron cuts a figure—but he is not figurative——" and, in speaking of Reynolds's parody of Wordsworth, he made the very significant remark, "I[t] would be just as well to trounce Lord Byron in the same manner." It can hardly be doubted that *The Cap and Bells* is, at least in part, an attempt to carry out this plan.

Up to a point, the similitude certainly holds. Elfinan is celebrated for his indiscriminate amours, which are the scandal of the nation. He is out of love with his bride before he even marries her, and is ready to deceive her before and after marriage. All this follows the pattern of Byron's disastrous marriage with Annabella Milbanke. Most certain evidence of all, Elfinan addresses Bellanaine, as he slips off invisible to meet Bertha Pearl, in these words:

> He bow'd at Bellanaine, and said—'Poor Bell!
> Farewell! farewell! and if for ever! still
> For ever fare thee well!'

This, as Mr. Middleton Murry has pointed out, is a direct quotation from the opening lines of Byron's poem to his wife on their separation in 1816

> Fare thee well! and if for ever,
> Still for ever, fare thee well:

There can be little doubt after this that part of Keats's intention was "to trounce Lord Byron" in the character of Elfinan.

Yet if that were the intention, it clearly fails in execution. Elfinan is not presented in any way that makes him a well-defined figure. Eban, Hum and Crafticanto are all larger and more convincing characters. He only displays anger, spite, and some conventional lovers' fears. He has no idiosyncrasies that in any way connect him with Byron. Nor does Bellanaine, though a somewhat waspish little creature, have anything that identifies her with Annabella Milbanke. In fact the poem, interpret it how we will, falls down badly when we come to what should have been its principal characters. Is there an explanation for this? One may be conjectured, and it is worth following since, if true, it may be a partial explanation also for the unsatisfactory nature of the whole poem. It lies, as so often with Keats, in the circumstances of his own life at this time.

It was for him a time of nervous strain and physical stress, noted by Charles Brown, and witnessed by the tone of his letters and of his poems to Fanny Brawne. It has its counterpart in the mysterious interlude of darkness and despair earlier in the year 1819, in the months of February and March. At that time, his doubts and fears, so far as they concerned his literary ability, took a very curious though understandable turn. They amounted to a comparison of his poetry and its neglect with Byron's and its success: it might almost be called a literary jealousy of Byron. He notes that Murray has sold 4,000 copies of Byron. He exclaims of himself, "You see what it is to be under six foot and not a lord"—i.e., Byron. Something of the same tone comes into his voice this autumn. Byron had this effect on less successful poets—admiration mixed with envy, even with a strange kind of self-identification. It may be remembered that John Clare, who was deeply moved by Byron, later thought, in his madness, that he *was* Byron. Keats spoke this autumn of the "immense difference" between himself and Byron. All the same, that he was drawn to make comparisons is itself significant. In the disturbed state of mind in which he wrote *The Cap and Bells*, one factor may not be so fantastic as it might appear at first sight. It is that Elfinan, as well as being Byron, is also, perhaps unknown to the poet, Keats himself.

There are several points at which this is indicated. One of the chief aspects of the otherwise lightly-sketched Elfinan is his small size—which, incidentally, puts this finally out of court as any portrait of "fat Regent". Elfinan throws "his little legs" upon the sofa, in his attitude of romantic lover, while Hum assures him that Bertha Pearl, though a mortal, will be a fit mate for the fairy Emperor

> since
> She's very delicate,—not over tall,—
> A fairy's hand, and in the waist why—very small.

Keats's obsession with his own small size has often been remarked upon, and it occurs again and again in his letters ("under six foot and not a lord"). He had also, in a lighter mood, satirised himself as the rhyming Dwarf in the extempore family verse to his brother George earlier in 1819

> When they were come into the Fairies Court

which has some other affinities with *The Cap and Bells*. Here Elfinan, like the Dwarf in the former poem, finds some relief from his predicament in poetry:

> For it may comfort and console him much,
> To rhyme and syllable his miseries;

while the two lincs that immediately follow are very important, since they point exactly to what his particular predicament in love was:

> Poor Elfinan! whose cruel fate was such,
> He sat and cursed a bride he knew he could not touch.

Elfinan's objection to Bellanaine is simply that she is a fairy, and therefore immaterial, and therefore unable to give him the sensual satisfaction to which he is accustomed from his earthly loves.

Now Keats, as has been said, was by now officially engaged to Fanny Brawne: but the engagement, instead of giving him calm or certainty, only seemed to cause intense agony of body and of mind. Part of his trouble undoubtedly was a thwarted desire for sensual satisfaction. In the summer, he had read one of the Arabian Tales in which men, when just about to embrace "a most enchanting lady", are thwarted of their desire. "How" he adds to Fanny, "I applied this to you, my dear." Elsewhere, he takes a slightly harsher note—"I am not one of the Paladins of old who liv'd upon water grass and smiles for years together" —while in the final bitterness of illness and his exile from England, he bursts out to Charles Brown,

> My dear Brown, I should have had her when I was in health, and I should have remained well.

There is evidence, too, that Fanny, partly alarmed by her passionate lover, partly perhaps counselled by a prudent and watchful mother, took care to keep him at a distance.

This means, then, that Bellanaine is Fanny: for that, there is some good evidence. Mr. Middleton Murry says, somewhat surprisingly, that Bellanaine is an anagram of Annabella—a statement that will at once be refuted by any crossword enthusiast. The name is a clear combination of Italian and French—bella naine—beautiful Dwarf, the exact counterpart of Keats himself, who styled himself as "the dwarf", and who had noted about Fanny when he first met her "She is about my height". Keats this autumn was in the throes, not only of thwarted sexual desire about Fanny, but of jealousy: it is to be remembered that the sub-title of the poem, which he preferred, was to be *The Jealousies*. The stanza which deals with Bellanaine's infidelities is particularly striking, when we compare it with what Keats himself wrote to Fanny.

> There he says plainly that she loved a man!
> That she around him, flutter'd, flirted, toy'd,
> Before her marriage with great Elfinan;
> That after marriage too, she never joy'd
> In husband's company, but still employ'd
> Her wits to 'scape away to Angle-land;
> Where liv'd the youth, who worried and annoy'd
> Her tender heart, and its warm ardours fann'd
> To such a dreadful blaze, her side would scorch her hand.

Keats in his *Ode to Fanny*, written at almost this exact time, has two stanzas:

> Why, this—you'll say, my Fanny! is not true:
> Put your soft hand upon your snowy side,
> Where the heart beats: confess—'tis nothing new—
> Must not a woman be
> A feather on the sea,
> Sway'd to and fro by every wind and tide?
> Of as uncertain speed
> As blow-ball from the mead?
>
> I know it—and to know it is despair
> To one who loves you as I love, sweet Fanny!
> Whose heart goes fluttering for you every where,
> Nor, when away you roam,
> Dare keep its wretched home,
> Love, Love alone, has pains severe and many:
> Then, loveliest! keep me free,
> From torturing jealousy.

The images and the feeling of these two pieces of description are almost identical. So too are Elfinan's feelings about his bride, when they are compared with passages that Keats was marking at this time in his copy of Burton's *The Anatomy of Melancholy*. Every remark against marriage gets an approving mark: every statement defending marriage gets from Keats a sarcastic query. He underlines heavily the statement

> The band of marriage is adamantine; no hope of loosing it; thou art undone.

In the poem, he makes Hum promise Elfinan

> You shall not throttled be in marriage noose;

and Elfinan's whole attitude is that, though ready for sensual adventure, he must get out of marriage at all costs.

It would be foolish to apply all this too exactly to Keats and Fanny, to the extent of seeking a Bertha for the one and a Hubert for the other, although it is interesting that Bertha is the heroine of Keats's unfinished *The Eve of St. Mark* (written February 13th–17th, 1819), even down to the "pleatings" of her dress. It is sufficient to observe that here at last is a reasonable explanation for the confused and unsatisfactory nature of the poem. Keats had intended it primarily as a literary satire, an attempt to adapt his own particular genius to some sort of literary journalism, by a parody of his brother writers, and by a fanciful portrayal of the rivalry between Lake Poets and Cockney School. He was diverted from this by his own harassed and obsessed love-situation. Like all people in a nervous and strained state of mind—and it must be guessed that he was near what we should call a nervous breakdown—he kept reverting to the one set of dominating thoughts which infected, like a disease, everything he did and everything he wrote. *The Cap and Bells*, even judged in its fragmentary state, fails because of an aim divided between the public and the personal. Indeed, until Keats could have cleared his mind of its personal obsessions, it is doubtful if he could have written more poetry. In this sense the doctors were right when they said his disease was largely of the mind; and it is the tragic role of the last poem that Keats wrote to demonstrate this dilemma.

VI

Can *The Cap and Bells* be dismissed, then, as something rather regrettable, an epilogue that we would rather not have, from a poet wasted by disease and personal worry into a shadow of his real creative self? This, as we began by saying, has been the common verdict; and although our discovery of the whole plan of literary satire, on which the poem was based, may increase its interest for us, we must admit that its lack of success decreases its value. Keats, whether writing for private amusement or for public entertainment, has simply not brought it off. Whether his mind was too blurred by personal stress, or whether he never was seriously enough interested in the design, we can never know.

Yet the poem has a virtue, and a unique one, perhaps outside the conscious will of its creator. It is, at any rate by fits and starts, the only poem that can be said to show the whole Keats, the Keats of the Letters, which many responsible critics have actually preferred to the Keats of the Collected Poems. When reading the letters, everyone is struck by the extraordinary comprehensive and resilient quality of Keats's mind. Every subject, grave or gay, is treated with the same gusto, and almost, sometimes, in the same breath. The sense of participation in all forms of life, nothing too immense or too trivial, ever-present in the letters, is somehow lacking, for all their greatness, in the poems. In his poetry, humour and grandeur are in separate compartments; domestic and occasional poetry is strictly divided from the poetry of high purpose. Only in scattered off-shoots of almost unconscious lyric spontaneity, such as *Meg Merrilies* or *La Belle Dame* do the two fuse for an immortal instant; and even they are not the whole Keats.

The Cap and Bells, with all its imperfections, is this Keats, the Keats of the Letters, the real chameleon poet, passing in an instant from puns to philosophy and back again—the poet noted by his friend Woodhouse, for whom everything had a life of its own, who could enter in imagination into the sensations even of such an object as a billiard-ball. The "innate universality", which he himself saw in Shakespeare, was Keats's highest ambition. In his letters, he shows it naturally. In his poems, it was still largely among those things "to come", after which he still felt himself straining. For all its faults, *The Cap and Bells* has at its best the universality and wide lively sympathy of the Letters, and what Keats himself called the "light and shade" necessary for poetry. A ready instance is his description of the City after hours, which echoes at once passages in his letters where he describes walking along Cheapside or the Poultry:

It was the time when wholesale houses close
Their shutters with a moody sense of wealth,
But retail dealers, diligent, let loose
The gas (objected to on score of health),
Convey'd in little solder'd pipes by stealth,
And make it flare in many a brilliant form . . .

The atmosphere is caught as completely as in Keats's famous prose description of the streets of Winchester in his letter that September. Again, the almost lyric passages of sensuous description of food and drink, which form a delightful part of many of Keats's letters, have their counterpart in the stanza which describes the pleasure taken by Hum in claret.

Whereat a narrow Flemish glass he took,
That once belong'd to Admiral De Witt,
Admired it with a connoisseuring look,
And with the ripest claret crowned it,
And, ere one lively bead could burst and flit,
He turn'd it quickly, nimbly upside down . . .

Here is the Keats who could enter into the nature of inanimate things, of food, drink, and the minor pleasures of life, with as much delight as in spiritual matters. Finally—and it is worth noting that such joyful descriptions come from a man whose letters at this time show the utmost despondency, there is the stanza of holiday:

The morn is full of holiday; loud bells
With rival clamours ring from every spire;
Cunningly-station'd music dies and swells
In echoing places; when the winds respire,
Light flags stream out like gauzy tongues of fire;
A metropolitan murmur, lifeful, warm,
Comes from the northern suburbs; rich attire
Freckles with red and gold the moving swarm;
While here and there clear trumpets blow a keen alarm.

For these alone, and many other small touches, we cannot regret *The Cap and Bells*. Every glimpse of the whole man is valuable; our only regret must be that it was a man, still whole enough to outward view, but inwardly attacked by the mysterious enemy of which this inconclusive poem is perhaps itself, though no longer so mysterious, a symbol.

APPENDIX A

KEATS'S MARKINGS IN HIS COPY OF THE *INFERNO*

HELL

CANTO I

Page 1

In the midway of this our mortal life,
I found me in a gloomy wood, astray
Gone from the path direct: and e'en to tell
It were no easy task, how savage wild
That forest, how robust and rough its growth,
Which to remember only, my dismay
Renews, in bitterness not far from death.
Yet to discourse of what there good befel,
All else will I relate discover'd there.
How first I enter'd it I scarce can say,
Such sleepy dulness in that instant weigh'd
My senses down, when the true path I left,
But when a mountain's foot I reach'd, where clos'd
The valley, that had pierc'd my heart with dread,
I look'd aloft, and saw his shoulders broad
Already vested with that planet's beam,
Who leads all wanderers safe through every way.
Then was a little respite to the fear,
That in my heart's recesses deep had lain,
All of that night, so pitifully pass'd:
And as a man, with difficult short breath,
Forespent with toiling, 'scap'd from sea to shore,
Turns to the perilous wide waste, and stands
At gaze; e'en so my spirit, that yet fail'd
Struggling with terror, turn'd to view the straits,
That none had pass'd and liv'd. My weary frame
After short pause recomforted, again

Page 2

| I journey'd on over that lonely steep,
||| The hinder foot still firmer. Scarce the ascent

Began, when, lo! a panther, nimble, light,
And cover'd with a speckled skin, appear'd,
Nor, when it saw me, vanish'd, rather strove
To check my onward going; that ofttimes
With purpose to retrace my steps I turn'd.
The hour was morning's prime, and on his way
Aloft the sun ascended with those stars,
That with him rose, when Love divine first mov'd
Those its fair works: so that with joyous hope
All things conspir'd to fill me, the gay skin
Of that swift animal, the matin dawn
And the sweet season. Soon that joy was chas'd,
And by new dread succeeded, when in view
A lion came, 'gainst me, as it appear'd,
With his head held aloft and hunger-mad,
That e'en the air was fear-struck. A she-wolf
Was at his heels, who in her leanness seem'd
Full of all wants, and many a land hath made
Disconsolate ere now. She with such fear
O'erwhelmed me, at the sight of her appall'd,
That of the height all hope I lost. As one,
Who with his gain elated, sees the time
When all unwares is gone, he inwardly
Mourns with heart-griping anguish; such was I,
Haunted by that fell beast, never at peace,
Who coming o'er against me, by degrees
Impell'd me where the sun in silence rests.
While to the lower space with backward step
I fell, my ken discern'd the form of one,
Whose voice seem'd faint through long disuse of speech.
When him in that great desert I espied,
"Have mercy on me!" cried I out aloud,
"Spirit! or living man! whate'er thou be!"

Page 4

Will lead thee hence through an eternal space,

Onward he mov'd, I close his steps pursu'd.

Canto IX

Page 35

The hue, which coward dread on my pale cheeks
Imprinted, when I saw my guide turn back,
Chas'd that from his which newly they had worn,

| And inwardly restrain'd it. He, as one
Who listens, stood attentive: for his eye
| Not far could lead him through the sable air,

Page 36

| Be shown, and thou shouldst view it, thy return
Upwards would be for ever lost." This said,
Himself my gentle master turn'd me round,
Nor trusted he my hands, but with his own
He also hid me. Ye of intellect

Page 37

| Thy visual nerve along that ancient foam,
There, thickest where the smoke ascends" As frogs
| Before their foe the serpent, through the wave
Ply swiftly all, till at the ground each one
Lies on a heap; more than a thousand spirits
| Destroy'd, so saw I fleeing before one
Who pass'd with unwet feet the Stygian sound.
He, from his face removing the gross air,

| This said, he turn'd back o'er the filthy way,
And syllable to us spake none, but wore
| The semblance of a man by other care

Page 38

| Beset, and keenly press'd, than thought of him

| Their lids all hung suspended, and beneath
From them forth issu'd lamentable moans,
| Such as the sad and tortur'd well might raise.

CANTO X

Page 39

| "O Tuscan! thou who through the city of fire
Alive art passing, so discreet of speech!
| Here please thee stay awhile. Thy utterance

Page 40

| Then, peering forth from the unclosed jaw,
Rose from his side a shade, high as the chin,

Leaning, methought, upon its knees uprais'd.
It look'd around, as eager to explore
If there were other with me; but perceiving
That fond imagination quench'd, with tears
Thus spake: "If thou through this blind prison go'st,

Page 41

I made ere my reply aware, down fell
Supine, nor after forth appear'd he more.
Meanwhile the other, great of soul, near whom
I yet was station'd, chang'd not count'nance stern,
Nor mov'd the neck, nor bent his ribbed side.

Such orisons ascend." Sighing he shook
The head, then thus resum'd: "In that affray

Page 42

So much of his large splendour yet imparts

"More than a thousand with me here are laid.
Within is Frederick, second of that name,
And the Lord Cardinal, and of the rest
I speak not." He, this said, from sight withdrew.
But I my steps toward the ancient bard
Reverting, ruminated on the words
Betokening me such ill. Onward he mov'd,
And thus in going question'd: "Whence the' amaze
That holds thy senses wrapt?" I satisfied
The' inquiry, and the sage enjoin'd me straight:
"Let thy safe memory store what thou hast heard
To thee importing harm; and note thou this,"
With his rais'd finger bidding me take heed,

Canto XI

Page 44

From the profound abyss, behind the lid
Of a great monument we stood retir'd,
Whereon this scroll I mark'd: "I have in charge
Pope Anastasius, whom Photinus drew
From the right path."—"Ere our descent behoves
We make delay, that somewhat first the sense,
To the dire breath accustom'd, afterward
Regard it not." My master thus; to whom
Answering I spake: "Some compensation find

Page 45

"Fraud, that in every conscience leaves a sting,

Page 46

But tell me this: they of the dull, fat pool,
Whom the rain beats, or whom the tempest drives,
Or who with tongues so fierce conflicting meet,

Not so accustom'd? or what other thoughts
Possess it? Dwell not in thy memory

"O Sun! who healest all imperfect sight,
Thou so content'st me, when thou solv'st my doubt,
That ignorance not less than knowledge charms.

Page 47

My steps on forward journey bent; for now
The Pisces play with undulating glance
Along the horizon, and the Wain lies all

CANTO XII

Page 48

The place where to descend the precipice
We came, was rough as Alp, and on its verge
Such object lay, as every eye would shun.
As is that ruin, which Adice's stream
On this side Trento struck, should'ring the wave,
Or loos'd by earthquake or for lack of prop;
For from the mountain's summit, whence it mov'd
To the low level, so the headlong rock
Is shiver'd, that some passage it might give
To him who from above would pass; e'en such
Into the chasm was that descent: and there
At point of the disparted ridge lay stretch'd
The infamy of Crete, detested brood
Of the feign'd heifer: and at sight of us
It gnaw'd itself, as one with rage distract.
To him my guide exclaim'd: "Perchance thou deem'st

That thou descend." Thus down our road we took
Through those dilapidated crags, that oft

Page 49

Mov'd underneath my feet, to weight like theirs
Unus'd. I pond'ring went, and thus he spake:
"Perhaps thy thoughts are of this ruin'd steep,

Had told. Between it and the rampart's base
On trail ran Centaurs, with keen arrows arm'd,
As to the chase they on the earth were wont.
At seeing us descend they each one stood;
And issuing from the troop, three sped with bows
And missile weapons chosen first; of whom
One cried from far: "Say to what pain ye come
Condemn'd, who down this steep have journied? Speak
From whence ye stand, or else the bow I draw."
To whom my guide: "Our answer shall be made
To Chiron, there, when nearer him we come.
Ill was thy mind, thus ever quick and rash."

Page 50

Then me he touch'd, and spake: "Nessus is this,
Who for the fair Deianira died,
And wrought himself revenge for his own fate.
He in the midst, that on his breast looks down,
Is the great Chiron who Achilles nurs'd;
That other Pholus, prone to wrath." Around
The foss these go by thousands, aiming shafts
At whatsoever spirit dares emerge
From out the blood, more than his guilt allows.
We to those beasts, that rapid strode along,
Drew near, when Chiron took an arrow forth,
And with the notch push'd back his shaggy beard
To the cheek-bone, then his great mouth to view
Exposing, to his fellows thus exclaim'd:
"Are ye aware, that he who comes behind
Moves what he touches? The feet of the dead
Are not so wont." My trusty guide, who now
Stood near his breast, where the two natures join,
Thus made reply: "He is indeed alive,
And solitary so must needs by me
Be shown the gloomy vale, thereto induc'd
By strict necessity, not by delight.
She left her joyful harpings in the sky,
Who this new office to my care consign'd.
He is no robber, no dark spirit I.

But by that virtue, which empowers my step
To tread so wild a path, grant us, I pray,
One of thy band, whom we may trust secure,
Who to the ford may lead us, and convey
Across, him mounted on his back; for he
Is not a spirit that may walk the air."
Then on his right breast turning, Chiron thus
To Nessus spake: "Return, and be their guide.
And if ye chance to cross another troop,
Command them keep aloof." Onward we mov'd,

Page 51

Whereon the hair so jetty clust'ring hangs,
Is Azzolino; that with flaxen locks

A race I next espied, who held the head,
And even all the bust, above the stream.

Canto XIII

Page 53

Ere Nessus yet had reach'd the other bank,
We enter'd on a forest, where no track
Of steps had worn a way. Not verdant there
The foliage, but of dusky hue; not light
The boughs and tapering, but with knares deform'd
And matted thick: fruits there were none, but thorns
Instead, with venom fill'd. Less sharp than these,
Less intricate the brakes, wherein abide
Those animals, that hate the cultur'd fields,
Betwixt Corneto and Cecina's stream.

As would my speech discredit." On all sides
I heard sad plainings breathe, and none could see
From whom they might have issu'd. In amaze

Page 54

From a great wilding gather'd I a branch,
And straight the trunk exclaim'd: "Why pluck'st thou me?"

Thy hand might well have spar'd us, had we been
The souls of serpents." As a brand yet green,
That burning at one end from the' other sends

A groaning sound, and hisses with the wind
That forces out its way, so burst at once
Forth from the broken splinter words and blood.
I, letting fall the bough, remain'd as one
Assail'd by terror, and the sage replied:
"If he, O injur'd spirit! could have believ'd
What he hath seen but in my verse describ'd,

Count it not grievous. I it was, who held
Both keys to Frederick's heart, and turn'd the wards,
Opening and shutting, with a skill so sweet,
That besides me, into his inmost breast
Scarce any other could admittance find.

Page 56

The dismal glade our bodies shall be hung,
Each on the wild thorn of his wretched shade."
Attentive yet to listen to the trunk
We stood, expecting farther speech, when us
A noise surpris'd, as when a man perceives
The wild boar and the hunt approach his place
Of station'd watch, who of the beasts and boughs
Loud rustling round him hears. And lo! there came
Two naked, torn with briers, in headlong flight,

And then, for that perchance no longer breath
Suffic'd him, of himself and of a bush
One group he made. Behind them was the wood
Full of black female mastiffs, gaunt and fleet,
As greyhounds that have newly slipp'd the leash.

CANTO XIV

Page 58

Soon as the charity of native land
Wrought in my bosom, I the scatter'd leaves
Collected, and to him restor'd, who now
Was hoarse with utt'rance. To the limit thence
We came, which from the third the second round

Each plant repell'd. The mournful wood waves round
Its garland on all sides, as round the wood
Spreads the sad foss. There, on the very edge,

Our steps we stay'd. It was an area wide
Of arid sand and thick, resembling most
The soil that erst by Cato's foot was trod.

Of naked spirits many a flock I saw,
All weeping piteously, to different laws
Subjected; for on the' earth some lay supine,
Some crouching close were seated, others pac'd
Incessantly around; the latter tribe,
More numerous, those fewer who beneath
The torment lay, but louder in their grief.
O'er all the sand fell slowly wafting down
Dilated flakes of fire, as flakes of snow
On Alpine summit, when the wind is hush'd.

Page 59

Unceasing was the play of wretched hands,
Now this, now that way glancing, to shake off
The heat, still falling fresh. I thus began:

To stop our entrance at the gate, say who
Is yon huge spirit, that, as seems, heeds not
The burning, but lies writhen in proud scorn,
As by the sultry tempest immatur'd?"

At their black smithy labouring by turns

Page 60

Next turning round to me with milder lip

Keep ever close." Silently on we pass'd
To where there gushes from the forest's bound
A little brook, whose crimson'd wave yet lifts
My hair with horror. As the rill, that runs

That having giv'n me appetite to know,
The food he too would give, that hunger crav'd.

Page 61

An ancient form there stands and huge, that turns
His shoulders towards Damiata, and at Rome
As in his mirror looks. Of finest gold

Canto XV

Page 63

One of the solid margins bears us now
Envelop'd in the mist, that from the stream
Arising, hovers o'er, and saves from fire
Both piers and water. As the Flemings rear
Their mound, 'twixt Ghent and Bruges, to chase back

They each one ey'd us, as at eventide
One eyes another under a new moon,
And toward us sharpen'd their sight as keen,
As an old tailor at his needle's eye.
Thus narrowly explor'd by all the tribe,
I was agniz'd of one, who by the skirt
Caught me, and cried, "What wonder have we here?"
And I, when he to me outstretch'd his arm,
Intently fix'd my ken on his parch'd looks,
That although smirch'd with fire, they hinder'd not
But I remember'd him; and towards his face
My hand inclining, answer'd: "Sir! Brunetto!

Page 64

I dar'd not from the path descend to tread
On equal ground with him, but held my head
Bent down, as one who walks in reverent guise.

Serene, I wander'd in a valley lost,
Before mine age had to its fulness reach'd.
But yester-morn I left it: then once more
Into that vale returning, him I met;
And by this path homeward he leads me back."

Ay and still smack of their rough mountain-flint,

Page 65

The dear, benign, paternal image, such
As thine was, when so lately thou didst teach me
The way for man to win eternity:

Page 66

Alike desist, for yonder I behold
A mist new-risen on the sandy plain.
A company with whom I may not sort,

Approaches. I commend my *Treasure* to thee,
Wherein I yet survive; my sole request."
  This said he turn'd, and seem'd as one of those,
Who o'er Verona's champain try their speed
For the green mantle, and of them he seem'd,
Not he who loses but who gains the prize.

CANTO XXII

Page 92

It hath been heretofore my chance to see
Horsemen with martial order shifting camp,
To onset sallying, or in muster rang'd,
Or in retreat sometimes outstretch'd for flight:
Light-armed squadrons and fleet foragers
Scouring thy plains, Arezzo! have I seen,
And clashing tournaments, and tilting jousts,
Now with the sound of trumpets, now of bells,
Tabors, or signals made from castled heights,
And with inventions multiform, our own,
Or introduc'd from foreign land; but ne'e
To such a strange recorder I beheld,
In evolution moving, horse nor foot,
Nor ship, that tack'd by sign from land or star.

Who burn'd within. As dolphins, that, in sign
To mariners, heave high their arched backs,
That thence forewarn'd they may advise to save
Their threaten'd vessel; so, at intervals,
To ease the pain his back some sinner show'd,
Then hid more nimbly than the lightning glance.
  Een as the frogs, that of a wat'ry moat
Stand at the brink, with the jaws only out,
Their feet and of the trunk all else conceal'd,
Thus on each part the sinners stood, but soon
As Barbariccia was at hand, so they

Page 93

Drew back under the wave. I saw, and yet
My heart doth stagger, one, that waited thus,
As it befals that oft one frog remains,
While the next springs away: and Graffiacan,
Who of the fiends was nearest, grappling seiz'd
His clotted locks, and dragg'd him sprawling up,
That he appear'd to me an otter. Each

Page 95

E'en thus the water-fowl, when she perceives
The falcon near, dives instant down, while he
Enrag'd and spent retires. That mockery
In Calcabrina fury stirr'd, who flew
After him, with desire of strife inflam'd;
And, for the barterer had 'scap'd, so turn'd
His talons on his comrade. O'er the dyke
In grapple close they join'd; but the 'other prov'd
A goshawk able to rend well his foe;

Canto XXIII

Page 97

In silence and in solitude we went,
One first, the other following his steps,
As minor friars journeying on their road.

And as one thought bursts from another forth,

He answer'd: "Were I form'd of leaded glass,
I should not sooner draw unto myself
Thy outward image, than I now imprint
That from within. This moment came thy thoughts

Page 98

He had not spoke his purpose to the end,
When I from far beheld them with spread wings
Approach to take us. Suddenly my guide
Caught me, ev'n as a mother that from sleep
Is by the noise arous'd, and near her sees
The climbing fires, who snatches up her babe
And flies ne'er pausing, careful more of him
Than of herself, that but a single vest
Clings round her limbs. Down from the jutting beach
Supine he cast him, to that pendent rock,
Which closes on one part the other chasm.

There in the depth we saw a painted tribe,
Who pac'd with tardy steps around, and wept,
Faint in appearance and o'ercome with toil.
Caps had they on, with hoods, that fell low down
Before their eyes, in fashion like to those
Worn by the monks in Cologne. Their outside

Page 99

We yet once more with them together turn'd
To leftward, on their dismal moan intent.
But by the weight oppress'd, so slowly came
The fainting people, that our company
Was chang'd at every movement of the step.

Ye who so swiftly speed through the dusk air.
Perchance from me thou shalt obtain thy wish."
Whereat my leader, turning, me bespake:
"Pause, and then onward at their pace proceed."
I staid, and saw two spirits in whose look

To other thus conferring said: "This one
Seems, by the action of his throat, alive.

The college of the mourning hypocrites,

And wear the body I have ever worn.

Page 100

Distorted, ruffling with deep sighs his beard.

CANTO XXIV

Page 102

In the year's early nonage, when the sun
Tempers his tresses in Aquarius' urn,
And now towards equal day the nights recede,
Whenas the rime upon the earth puts on
Her dazzling sister's image, but not long
Her milder sway endures, then riseth up
The village hind, whom fails his wintry store,
And looking out beholds the plain around
All whiten'd, whence impatiently he smites
His thighs, and to his hut returning in,
There paces to and fro, wailing his lot,
As a discomfited and helpless man;
Then comes he forth again, and feels new hope
Spring in his bosom, finding e'en thus soon
The world hath chang'd its count'nance, grasps his crook,

Page 103

"For not on downy plumes, nor under shade
Of canopy reposing, fame is won,
Without which whosoe'er consumes his days
Leaveth such vestige of himself on earth,
As smoke in air or foam upon the wave.

Narrower and steeper far to climb. From talk
I ceas'd not, as we journey'd, so to seem
Least faint; whereat a voice from the 'other foss

Page 104

Yet shrinks the vital current. Of her sands
Let Lybia vaunt no more: if Jaculus,
Pareas and Chelyder be her brood,
Cenchris and Amphisboena, plagues so dire
Or in such numbers swarming ne'er she shew'd,
Not with all Ethiopia, and whate'er
Above the Erythraean sea is spawn'd.
Amid this dread exuberance of woe
Ran naked spirits wing'd with horrid fear,
Nor hope had they of crevice where to hide,
Or heliotrope to charm them out of view.

And, where the neck is on the shoulders tied,
Transpierc'd him. Far more quickly than e'er pen
Wrote O or I, he kindled, burn'd, and chang'd
To ashes all, pour'd out upon the earth.
When there dissolv'd he lay, the dust again

Page 105

Uproll'd spontaneous, and the self same form
Instant resum'd. So mighty sages tell,
The' Arabian Phoenix, when five hundred years
Have well nigh circled, dies, and springs forthwith
Renascent. Blade nor herb throughout his life
He tastes, but tears of frankincense alone
And odorous amomum: swaths of nard
And myrrh his funeral shroud. As one that falls,
He knows not how, by force demoniac dragg'd

"It grieves me more to have been caught by thee
In this sad plight, which thou beholdest, than
When I was taken from the other life.

Canto XXV

Page 108

|| A hundred blows, and not the tenth was felt."

Should stand attentive, plac'd against my lips
The finger lifted. If, O reader! now
Thou be not apt to credit what I tell,
No marvel; for myself do scarce allow
The witness of mine eyes. But as I look'd
Toward them, lo! a serpent with six feet
Springs forth on one, and fastens full upon him:
His midmost grasp'd the belly, a forefoot
Seiz'd on each arm (while deep in either cheek
He flesh'd his fangs); the hinder on the thighs
Were spread, 'twixt which the tail inserted curl'd
Upon the reins behind. Ivy ne'er clasp'd
A dodder'd oak, as round the other's limbs
The hideous monster intertwin'd his own.
Then, as they both had been of burning wax,
Each melted into other, mingling hues,
That which was either now was seen no more.
Thus up the shrinking paper, ere it burns,
A brown tint glides, not turning yet to black,
And the clean white expires. The other two
Look'd on exclaiming: "Ah, how dost thou change,
Agnello! See! Thou art nor double now,
Nor only one." The two heads now become
One, and two figures blended in one form

Page 109

Appear'd, where both were lost. Of the four lengths
Two arms were made: the belly and the chest
The thighs and legs into such members chang'd
As never eye hath seen. Of former shape
All trace was vanish'd. Two yet neither seem'd
That image miscreate, and so pass'd on
With tardy steps. As underneath the scourge
Of the fierce dog star, that lays bare the fields,
Shifting from brake to brake, the lizard seems
A flash of lightning, if he thwart the road,
So toward th' entrails of the other two
Approaching seem'd, an adder all on fire,
As the dark pepper-grain, livid and swart.
In that part, whence our life is nourish'd first,
One he transpiere'd; then down before him fell

Stretch'd out. The pierced spirit look'd on him
But spake not; yea stood motionless and yawn'd,
As if by sleep or fev'rous fit assail'd.
He ey'd the serpent, and the serpent him.
One from the wound, the other from the mouth
Breath'd a thick smoke, whose vap'ry columns join'd.

Page 110

Not yet their glaring and malignant lamps
Were shifted, though each feature chang'd beneath.

He, on the earth who lay, meanwhile extends
His sharpen'd visage, and draws down the ears
Into the head, as doth the slug his horns.

Canto XXVI

Page 112

Are of the truth presageful, thou ere long

Pursuing thus our solitary way
Among the crags and splinters of the rock,
Sped not our feet without the help of hands.
  Then sorrow seiz'd me, which e'en now revives,
As my thought turns again to what I saw,
And, more than I am wont, I rein and curb
The powers of nature in me, lest they run
Where Virtue guides not; that if aught of good
My gentle star, or something better gave me,
I envy not myself the precious boon.
  As in that season, when the sun least veils
His face that lightens all, what time the fly
Gives way to the shrill gnat, the peasant then

Page 113

Upon some cliff reclin'd, beneath him sees
Fire-flies innumerous spangling o'er the vale,
Vineyard or tilth, where his day-labour lies:
With flames so numberless throughout its space
Shone the eighth chasm, apparent, when the depth

And grasp'd a flinty mass, or else had fall'n,
Though push'd not from the height. The guide, who mark'd
How I did gaze attentive, thus began:
"Within these ardours are the spirits, each

To ask thee, who is in yon fire, that comes
So parted at the summit, as it seem'd
Ascending from that funeral pile, where lay
The Theban brothers?" He replied: "Within

Page 114

To pause, till here the horned flame arrive.

Of the old flame forthwith the greater horn
Began to roll, murmuring, as a fire
That labours with the wind, then to and fro
Wagging the top, as a tongue uttering sounds,
Threw out its voice, and spake: "When I escap'd

Page 115

The walls of Seville to my right I left,
On the 'other hand already Cecuta past.
'O brothers!' I began, 'who to the west
'Through perils without number now have reach'd,
'To this the short remaining watch, that yet
'Our senses have to wake, refuse not proof
'Of the unpeopled world, following the track
'Of Phoebus. Call to mind from whence ye sprang:
'Ye were not form'd to live the life of brutes,
'But virtue to pursue and knowledge high.'
With these few words I sharpen'd for the voyage
The mind of my associates, that I then
Could scarcely have withheld them. To the dawn
Our poop we turn'd, and for the witless flight
Made our oars wings, still gaining on the left.
Each star of the 'other pole night now beheld,
And ours so low, that from the ocean-floor
It rose not. Five times re-illum'd, as oft
Vanish'd the light from underneath the moon
Since the deep way we enter'd, when from far
Appear'd a mountain dim, loftiest methought

Page 116

Of all I e'er beheld. Joy seiz'd us straight,
But soon to mourning chang'd. From the new land
A whirlwind sprung, and at her foremost side
Did strike the vessel. Thrice it whirl'd her round
With all the waves, the fourth time lifted up
The poop, and sank the prow: so fate decreed:
And over us the booming billow clos'd."

Canto XXVII

Page 118

Is steadfast. There Polenta's eagle broods,
And in his broad circumference of plume
O'ershadows Cervia. The green talons grasp

Where they are wont, an augre of their fangs.

Under the lion of the snowy lair.

Page 119

Long as this spirit mov'd the bones and pulp
My mother gave me, less my deeds bespake

Reach'd the world's limit. Soon as to that part
Of life I found me come, when each behoves
To lower sails and gather in the lines;

In himself, rev'renc'd, nor in me that cord,
Which us'd to mark with leanness whom it girded.

Page 120

"When I was number'd with the dead, then came
Saint Francis for me; but a cherub dark
He met, who cried; 'Wrong me not; he is mine,

'E'er since I watch'd him, hov'ring at his hair.

APPENDIX B

POEMS OR PASSAGES OF KEATS'S POETRY INFLUENCED BY HIS READING OF THE *INFERNO*

On Visiting the Tomb of Burns

The Town, the churchyard, and the setting sun,
The clouds, the trees, the rounded hills all seem,
Though beautiful, cold—strange—as in a dream,
I dreamed long ago, now new begun.
The short-liv'd paly Summer is but won
From Winter's ague, for one hour's gleam;
Though sapphire-warm, their stars do never beam:
All is cold Beauty; pain is never done:
For who has mind to relish, Minos-wise,
The Real of Beauty, free from that dead hue
Sickly imagination and sick pride
Cast wan upon it? Burns! with honour due
I oft have honour'd thee. Great shadow, hide
Thy face; I sin against thy native skies.

* * * *

HYPERION

A Fragment

Book I
lines 1–25

Deep in the shady sadness of a vale
Far sunken from the healthy breath of morn,
Far from the fiery noon, and eve's one star,
Sat gray-hair'd Saturn, quiet as a stone,
Still as the silence round about his lair;
Forest on forest hung about his head
Like cloud on cloud. No stir of air was there,
Not so much life as on a summer's day
Robs not one light seed from the feather'd grass,
But where the dead leaf fell, there did it rest.
A stream went voiceless by, still deadened more
By reason of his fallen divinity
Spreading a shade: the Naiad 'mid her reeds
Press'd her cold finger closer to her lips.

Along the margin-sand large foot-marks went,
No further than to where his feet had stray'd,
And slept there since. Upon the sodden ground
His old right hand lay nerveless, listless, dead,
Unsceptred; and his realmless eyes were closed;
While his bow'd head seem'd list'ning to the Earth,
His ancient mother, for some comfort yet.

It seem'd no force could wake him from his place:
But there came one, who with a kindred hand
Touch'd his wide shoulders, after bending low
With reverence, though to one who knew it not.

Book I
lines 343–357

Be thou therefore in the van
Of Circumstance; yea, seize the arrow's barb
Before the tense string murmur.—To the earth!
For there thou wilt find Saturn, and his woes.
Meantime I will keep watch on thy bright sun,
And of thy seasons be a careful nurse.'—
Ere half this region-whisper had come down,
Hyperion arose, and on the stars
Lifted his curved lids, and kept them wide
Until it ceas'd; and still he kept them wide:
And still they were the same bright, patient stars.
Then with a slow incline of his broad breast,
Like to a diver in the pearly seas,
Forward he stoop'd over the airy shore,
And plung'd all noiseless into the deep night.

Book II
lines 1–17

Just at the self-same beat of Time's wide wings
Hyperion slid into the rustled air,
And Saturn gain'd with Thea that sad place
Where Cybele and the bruised Titans mourn'd.
It was a den where no insulting light
Could glimmer on their tears; where their own groans
They felt, but heard not, for the solid roar
Of thunderous waterfalls and torrents hoarse,
Pouring a constant bulk, uncertain where.
Crag jutting forth to crag, and rocks that seem'd
Ever as if just rising from a sleep,

Forehead to forehead held their monstrous horns;
And thus in thousand hugest phantasies
Made a fit roofing to this nest of woe.
Instead of thrones, hard flint they sat upon,
Couches of rugged stone, and slaty ridge
Stubborn'd with iron.

* * * *

On A Dream

As Hermes once took to his feathers light,
When lulled Argus, baffled, swoon'd and slept,
So on a Delphic reed, my idle spright
So play'd, so charm'd, so conquer'd, so bereft
The dragon-world of all its hundred eyes;
And, seeing it asleep, so fled away,
Not to pure Ida with its snow-cold skies,
Nor unto Tempe, where Jove griev'd that day;
But to that second circle of sad hell,
Where in the gust, the whirlwind, and the flaw
Of rain and hail-stones, lovers need not tell
Their sorrows,—pale were the sweet lips I saw,
Pale were the lips I kiss'd, and fair the form
I floated with, about that melancholy storm.

* * * *

La Belle Dame Sans Merci

I

O what can ail thee, knight-at-arms,
Alone and palely loitering?
The sedge is wither'd from the lake,
And no birds sing.

II

O what can ail thee, knight-at-arms,
So haggard and so woe-begone?
The squirrel's granary is full,
And the harvest's done.

III

I see a lily on thy brow
  With anguish moist and fever dew;
And on thy cheek a fading rose
  Fast withereth too.

IV

I met a lady in the meads,
  Full beautiful—a faery's child,
Her hair was long, her foot was light,
  And her eyes were wild.

V

I made a garland for her head,
  And bracelets too, and fragrant zone;
She look'd at me as she did love,
  And made sweet moan.

VI

I set her on my pacing steed,
  And nothing else saw all day long,
For sideways would she bend, and sing
  A faery's song.

VII

She found me roots of relish sweet,
  And honey wild, and manna dew;
And sure in language strange she said—
  'I love thee true!'

VIII

She took me to her elfin grot,
  And there she gazed and sigh'd full sore,
And there I shut her wild wild eyes
  With kisses four.

IX

And there she lulled me asleep,
  And there I dream'd—Ah! woe betide!
The latest dream I ever dream'd
  On the cold hill side.

X

I saw pale kings and princes too,
  Pale warriors, death-pale were they all;
They cried—'La Belle Dame sans Merci
  Hath thee in thrall!'

XI

I saw their starv'd lips in the gloam,
  With horrid warning gaped wide,
And I awoke, and found me here,
  On the cold hill side.

XII

And this is why I sojourn here,
  Alone and palely loitering,
Though the sedge is wither'd from the lake,
  And no birds sing.

* * * *

To Sleep

O soft embalmer of the still midnight,
  Shutting, with careful fingers and benign,
Our gloom-pleas'd eyes, embower'd from the light,
  Enshaded in forgetfulness divine;
O soothest Sleep! if so it please thee, close
  In midst of this thine hymn, my willing eyes,
Or wait the Amen, ere thy poppy throws
  Around my bed its lulling charities;
  Then save me, or the passed day will shine
Upon my pillow, breeding many woes,—
    Save me from curious conscience, that still lords
Its strength for darkness, burrowing like a mole;
  Turn the key deftly in the oiled wards,
And seal the hushed casket of my soul.

* * * *

King Stephen

A Fragment of a Tragedy

ACT I, SCENE II.—*Another Part of the Field.*

Trumpets sounding a Victory.
Enter Glocester, *Knights, and Forces.*

Glocester. Now may we lift our bruised visors up,
And take the flattering freshness of the air,
While the wide din of battle dies away
Into times past, yet to be echoed sure
In the silent pages of our chroniclers.
First Knight. Will Stephen's death be mark'd there, my good Lord,
Or that we gave him lodging in yon towers?
Glocester. Fain would I know the great usurper's fate.

Enter two Captains severally.

First Captain. My Lord!
Second Captain. Most noble Earl!
First Captain. The King—
Second Captain. The Empress greets—
Glocester. What of the King?
First Captain. He sole and lone maintains
A hopeless bustle mid our swarming arms,
And with a nimble savageness attacks,
Escapes, makes fiercer onset, then anew
Eludes death, giving death to most that dare
Trespass within the circuit of his sword!
He must by this have fallen. Baldwin is taken;
And for the Duke of Bretagne, like a stag
He flies, for the Welsh beagles to hunt down.
God save the Empress!
Glocester. Now our dreaded Queen:
What message from her Highness?
Second Captain. Royal Maud
From the throng'd towers of Lincoln hath look'd down,
Like Pallas from the walls of Ilion,
And seen her enemies havock'd at her feet.
She greets most noble Gloster from her heart,
Intreating him, his captains, and brave knights,
To grace a banquet. The high city gates
Are envious which shall see your triumph pass;
The streets are full of music.

Enter Second Knight.

Glocester. Whence come you?
Second Knight. From Stephen, my good Prince,—Stephen! Stephen!
Glocester. Why do you make such echoing of his name?
Second Knight. Because I think, my lord, he is no man,
But a fierce demon, 'nointed safe from wounds,
And misbaptized with a Christian name.
Glocester. A mighty soldier!—Does he still hold out?
Second Knight. He shames our victory. His valour still
Keeps elbow-room amid our eager swords,
And holds our bladed falchions all aloof—
His gleaming battle-axe being slaughter-sick,
Smote on the morion of a Flemish knight,
Broke short in his hand; upon the which he flung
The heft away with such a vengeful force,
It paunch'd the Earl of Chester's horse, who then
Spleen-hearted came in full career at him.
Glocester. Did no one take him at a vantage then?
Second Knight. Three then with tiger leap upon him flew,
Whom, with his sword swift-drawn and nimbly held,
He stung away again, and stood to breathe,
Smiling. Anon upon him rush'd once more
A throng of foes, and in this renew'd strife,
My sword met his and snapp'd off at the hilts.
Glocester. Come, lead me to this Mars—and let us move
In silence, not insulting his sad doom
With clamorous trumpets. To the Empress bear
My salutation as befits the time.

(*Exeunt* GLOCESTER *and Forces.*)

SCENE III.—*The Field of Battle.*

Enter STEPHEN *unarmed.*

A cancelled opening to this scene, in Keats's hand, reads

Stephen. Another Sword! for one short minute longer
That I may papper (*sic*) that De Kaimes and then
Yield to some twenty squadrons—Stephen say
Wouldst thou exchange this helmeted renown
To rule in qu(i)et Pylos Nestor-like?
No!—
Enter De Kaims Knights and Soldiers dropping in.

* * * *

The Fall of Hyperion

A Dream

Canto One
lines 97–153

When in midday the sickening East-Wind
Shifts sudden to the South, the small warm rain
Melts out the frozen incense from all flowers,
And fills the air with so much pleasant health
That even the dying man forgets his shroud;
Even so that lofty sacrificial fire,
Sending forth Maian incense, spread around
Forgetfulness of everything but bliss,
And clouded all the altar with soft smoke;
From whose white fragrant curtains thus I heard
Language pronounced: 'If thou canst not ascend
These steps, die on that marble where thou art.
Thy flesh, near cousin to the common dust,
Will parch for lack of nutriment; thy bones
Will wither in few years, and vanish so
That not the quickest eye could find a grain
Of what thou now art on that pavement cold.
The sands of thy short life are spent this hour,
And no hand in the universe can turn
Thy hourglass, if these gummed leaves be burnt
Ere thou canst mount up these immortal steps.'
I heard, I look'd: two senses both at once
So fine, so subtle, felt the tyranny
Of that fierce threat and the hard task proposed.
Prodigious seem'd the toil; the leaves were yet
Burning, when suddenly a palsied chill
Struck from the paved level up my limbs,
And was ascending quick to put cold grasp
Upon those streams that pulse beside the throat.
I shriek'd, and the sharp anguish of my shriek
Stung my own ears; I strove hard to escape
The numbness, strove to gain the lowest step.
Slow, heavy, deadly was my pace: the cold
Grew stifling, suffocating at the heart;
And when I clasp'd my hands I felt them not.
One minute before death my iced foot touch'd
The lowest stair; and, as it touch'd, life seem'd
To pour in at the toes; I mounted up
As once fair Angels on a ladder flew
From the green turf to heaven. 'Holy Power,'

Cried I, approaching near the horned shrine,
'What am I that should so be saved from death?
What am I that another death come not
To choke my utterance, sacrilegious, here?'
Then said the veiled shadow: 'Thou hast felt
What 'tis to die and live again before
Thy fated hour; that thou hadst power to do so
Is thine own safety; thou hast dated on
Thy doom.' 'High Prophetess,' said I, 'purge off,
Benign, if so it please thee, my mind's film.'
'None can usurp this height,' returned that shade,
' But those to whom the miseries of the world
Are misery, and will not let them rest.
All else who find a haven in the world,
Where they may thoughtless sleep away their days,
If by a chance into this fane they come,
Rot on the pavement where thou rottedst half.'

* * * *

To Autumn

I

Season of mists and mellow fruitfulness!
  Close bosom-friend of the maturing sun;
Conspiring with him how to load and bless
  With fruit the vines that round the thatch-eves run;
To bend with apples the moss'd cottage-trees,
  And fill all fruit with ripeness to the core;
  To swell the gourd, and plump the hazel shells
  With a sweet kernel; to set budding more,
And still more, later flowers for the bees,
Until they think warm days will never cease,
    For summer has o'er-brimm'd their clammy cells.

II

Who hath not seen thee oft amid thy store?
  Sometimes whoever seeks abroad may find
Thee sitting careless on a granary floor,
  Thy hair soft-lifted by the winnowing wind;
Or on a half-reap'd furrow sound asleep,
  Drows'd with the fume of poppies, while thy hook
    Spares the next swath and all its twined flowers:

And sometimes like a gleaner thou dost keep
  Steady thy laden head across a brook;
  Or by a cyder-press, with patient look,
    Thou watchest the last oozings hours by hours.

III

Where are the songs of Spring? Ay, where are they?
  Think not of them, thou hast thy music too,—
While barred clouds bloom the soft-dying day,
  And touch the stubble-plains with rosy hue;
Then in a wailful choir the small gnats mourn
  Among the river sallows, borne aloft
    Or sinking as the light wind lives or dies;
And full-grown lambs loud bleat from hilly bourn;
  Hedge-crickets sing; and now with treble soft
  The red-breast whistles from a garden-croft;
    And gathering swallows twitter in the skies

APPENDIX C

KEATS'S LETTERS OF OCTOBER 26th / 27th, 1818, *TROILUS AND CRESSIDA* AND A LETTER TO TOM KEATS

OCTOBER 26TH / 27TH 1818 (Letter 93)	*Troilus and Cressida* (Marked passages)	LETTER TO TOM KEATS (Letter 71)
which seem to point like indices into the midst of the whole pro and con	And in such Indexes, although small prickes To their subsequent Volumes I. III. 343–4	
the wordsworthian or egotistical sublime;		Lord Wordsworth
which is a thing per se and stands alone	They say he is a very man per se and stands alone I. II. 15	
it is not itself—it has no self . . . not myself goes home to myself:	For speculation turnes not to it selfe, Till it hath trauail'd, and is married there Where it may see it selfe; III. III. 109–111	
I will assay to reach to as high a summit in Poetry as the nerve bestowed upon me will suffer. The faint conceptions I have of poems to come brings the blood frequently into my forehead.	Nerve, and Bone of Greece I. III. 58 *Keats's note on same page* "His plans of tasks to come were not of this world . . . how tremendous must have been his Conception of Ultimates."	
the solitary indifference I feel for applause even from the finest Spirits,		that mass of beauty which is harvested from these grand materials, by the finest spirits,

October 26th 1818 (Letter 94)	*Troilus and Cressida* (Marked passages)	Letter to Tom Keats (Letter 71)
the chairs and Sofa stuffed with Cygnet's down;	to whose soft seizure, The Cignets Downe is harsh, I. I. 59–60	
the Window opening on Winander mere,		along the border of Winandermere *and* (Letter 73) his parlor window looks directly down Winandermere;
The mighty abstract Idea I have of Beauty in all things		the abstract endeavour of being able to add a mite to that mass of beauty
I feel . . . , as my imagination strengthens, that I do not live in this world alone		I live in the eye; and my imagination, surpassed, is at rest—
"I wander, like a lost Soul upon the stygian Banks staying for waftage,"	I stalke about her doore Like a strange soule upon the Stigian bankes Staying for waftage. III. II. 9–11	
the generallity of women	the general sex| V. II, 129	

NOTE

It would, I think, be both discourteous and disingenuous for me not to mention in this book Mr. Middleton Murry's attack on the critical methods of my previous book, *John Keats: The Living Year*. Mr. Murry is one of our most distinguished and original contributors to our knowledge and understanding of Keats; tributes to him will be found throughout these studies. In his forty-page essay 'Keats and Isabella Jones', contained in his *Keats* (Jonathan Cape, 1955), he goes, however, far beyond the stated purpose of his essay, and attempts to discredit not only my whole critical method of dating Keats's poems but also those critics who have, in reviewing my book, accepted it.

It would be equally impossible and unprofitable to answer the numerous minute points he raises in this essay, detail by detail. At one moment, however, he seems to imply that my whole critical method in *The Living Year* was contrived so that I might date the first draft of Keats's *Bright Star* earlier than other critics have imagined, and so bring it into juxtaposition with Keats's romantic encounter with Mrs. Isabella Jones. This, I must assure Mr. Murry, is not the case. I had adopted my method and dated *Bright Star* by it long before any proof emerged that the enigmatic "lady from Hastings", whom Keats re-encountered in October 1818, was, or had anything to do with, Mrs. Isabella Jones. His groundless suspicions on this point have led me to examine *Bright Star* in the present essay without any reference whatsoever to Mrs. Jones; I hope this will be accepted as evidence of my honesty of purpose in this matter.

INDEX

of persons, books and poems